ANCESTORS AND DESCENDANTS OF

ASAHEL, JR. AND MARY (SMEDLEY)

FOOTE

OF WILLIAMSTOWN MA

1804 - 1882

BY JUDITH BENNETT WILSON

Ancestors and Descendants of Asahel, Jr. and Mary (Smedley) Foote of Williamstown MA 1804 – 1882.

ISBN 978-0692574126

Library of Congress Control Number: 2016954143

The Foote Family Coat of Arms, and an edited gedcom of the Asahel Foote, Jr. line, are courtesy of the Foote Family Association of America and Rebecca F. S. Owens. Updated data on the Nathaniel Foote line through Asahel, Sr. are courtesy of Ellwood Count Curtis' The Descendants of Nathaniel Foote (1592 – 1644) and Elizabeth Deming (c. 1595 – 1683).

The staff and volunteers at the Lee Library, the Berkshire Athenaeum, Pittstown MA, and the Williamstown Historic Museum were all of immeasurable assistance.

Layout by Lese Dunton.

Printed by CreateSpace, an Amazon.com Company.

DEDICATION

George W. Clapp, Avalon NJ in the 1970s.

Gentleman, scholar
and the best uncle ever!

Loyalty and Truth

Foote Coat of Arms

There are various versions of a legend in which King Charles II of England was hidden in an oak tree by Nathaniel Foote to save him from Cromwell after the Battle of Worcester on 3 Sep 1651. The story was repeated in serious family histories until it was finally pointed out that Nathaniel had emigrated to Watertown, Massachusetts when Charles was only four years old, and had been dead for almost seven years when the Battle of Worcester took place.

"Nathaniel Foote, moreover, was a Puritan, and if he had been in England at the time, and alive, he would have been on Cromwell's side. It's too bad; they enjoy the story in Berkshire[9-136]." Regardless, the Foote Family Association in America continues to use a coat-of-arms featuring the oak tree, allegedly bestowed in gratitude by King Charles II, along with Nathaniel's land grant in Massachusetts!

TABLE OF CONTENTS

PART I – THE FOOTES

PART II – THE SMEDLEYS
(to come)

FOREWORD

In the early 1970s, George Wirt Clapp began compiling family histories about his wife's four pairs of great-grandparents. He completed books about three couples during his lifetime. The fourth, Deacon Asahel Foote, Jr. and his wife, Mary Smedley, were left until last, as that family line had almost entirely died out. His niece, Judith Bennett Wilson, in whose care he left much of his research, has undertaken this final project.

Both the Footes and the Smedleys arrived in the Boston area in the 1630s, then migrated through CT, as far as its southern coast. Genealogists have long noted that many founding families actually seemed to possess a "migratory" gene, which certainly appears true of the Foote/Smedley clan. Both families eventually returned north, and not long before the American Revolution, they had settled in the Berkshires.

The lives of Asahel and Mary's grandparents and parents begin the narratives of the Foote (Part I) and Smedley (Part II) lines. Both families were prominent citizens of the towns they helped establish (Lee and Williamstown MA, respectively). The story of Asahel's and Mary's lives in Williamstown completes Part I.

Their son, Charles Rollin, and his wife, Sarah Cole, and their migration to southern California in the 1870s, were well detailed in George Clapp's 2002 book: Ancestors and Descendants of Harvey Towner and Caroline (Waterman) Cole of Williamstown MA 1810 - 1881 (ISBN 0-9718988-0-4). The Cole/Waterman book also contains an in-depth discussion of life in colonial New England, along with a vivid picture of life in mid-19th century Williamstown.

Five generations of Charles Rollin and Sarah (Cole) Foote's descendants were also enumerated in the Cole/Waterman book, so that information is not repeated here. Perhaps individual families will want to note in their copies of the Cole/Waterman book any marriages, births and deaths that have occurred since 2002.

Following the narrative sections in Parts I and II are Register Reports (the widely accepted standard format of the New England Historic Genealogical Society), detailing the ancestral lines of the Footes and Smedleys from their arrival in the New World in the 1630s. These reports replace many of the charts and indices contained in the three volumes compiled by George Clapp.

Each part concludes with a selection of photos and illustrations, both contemporary and historical, and a list of sources

Not only have many research files been compiled by various family members about the Footes and Smedleys, many letters, pamphlets, bibles and other memorabilia also exist. When Judith Bennett Wilson determines that she is too old to properly care for them, they will reside in a climate-controlled archive at the New England Historic Genealogical Society in Boston, where any and all family members, as well as others who may have an interest in this Foote/Smedley line, will have easy access to them.

NOTES ABOUT SOURCES AND FORMAT

With so much undocumented and/or erroneous information available on the internet, accurate source citations are vital in creating a respectable family history. Digging them up is also the most tedious aspect of such a project!

Fortunately, Rebecca Owens, Genealogist for the Foote Family Association of America was willing to review and improve the database I compiled in Reunion (the genealogy software for Macintosh), so it is consistent with the best available current information.

Foote genealogists are also fortunate that Abram Foote's definitive <u>Foote Family Comprising the Genealogy and History of Nathaniel Foote of Wethersfield, Conn. and his Descendants</u> Volume I, 1907 and Volume II, 1932 is fairly reliable, compared with many others also compiled at the turn of the 20th century (when compiling family histories was a very popular undertaking). However, it contains very few source notes.

Luckily, Elwood Count Curtis, the author of many other reputable compilations about early New England families, recently produced an updated version of Abram Foote's first four generations. Where available, he used the latest version of the Barbour collection, the official records of the state of CT, to corroborate (or fix) Abram Foote's information. This work is the source of all material for the first four generations in the Foote Ancestor Register Report (FARR), unless otherwise noted.

For the next three generations, which Curtis has not yet updated, a combination of the Abram Foote books, vital records, and other locally available sources, plus a bit of family recollection, have been employed. A "Farmer's Journal" was kept by Asahel Foote between 1841 and 1868, which corroborates or corrects some of the published dates of his many accomplishments. A list of all Part I Foote sources follows the Foote Ancestor Register Report, which in turn follows the three-generation narrative about Asahel, Jr, his father, Asahel, Sr. and his grandfather, Jonathan Foote.

A similar turn of the century genealogy of the Smedley family by Gilbert Cope forms the basis of the Smedlely Ancestor Register Report (SARR), along with an online gedcom whose accuracy has been extensively verified. The same format of a narrative about Mary and her father and grandfather, followed by a formal Register Report, illustrations and a source list comprises Part II, the Smedley section of the book.

In any instance when family legend has been relied on, that fact is clearly noted. But as with George Clapp's earlier works, citations are generally not provided for dates and anecdotes about generations whose vital records are a matter of recent family memory.

To simplify source citations, page numbers are not included when the source is organized alphabetically or chronologically, which makes it quite easy to find a specific record without knowing its page number. If only one source note is provided for an individual, the person's other vital records have also come from that source.

THE FOOTE* FAMILY LINE, FROM JONATHAN TO ASAHEL, JR.

Jonathan Foote, 1715 – 1803, Asahel, Jr.'s Grandfather

The first description of a religious service in Lee MA claims it was held in Oliver West's barn on 8 January 1778. The haymow served as the singers' gallery, where six of Jonathan and Sarah Foote's eight children held forth as the choir, described by town poet and wit, Nathan Dillingham:

> *David and Ase sung bass;*
> *Jonathan and Fenner sang tenor;*
> *'Vice and Sol beat them all[28-138]."*

When Jonathan Foote moved from Colchester CT to Lee MA in 1770, he was already 55 years old, and his seven unmarried children ranged in age from 18 to 2[1]. (His oldest daughter was already married[13].) He was a signer of the 1774 petition that led to the eventual incorporation of the town[28-133]. It is assumed the family lived in a log cabin on Jonathan's property until 1778, when he built a big house (still in use as a B&B) at the top of a hill on the east side of town[15].

As the story goes, half way up the street to Jonathan's house was the town cemetery. Logically, the access road was referred to as Cemetery Street. Not being too keen on this as his street address, Jonathan's great-grandson, Theron Lyman Foote, who inherited the house in the mid-19th century, cut a deal with the town: he would plant maple trees from the bottom of the hill all the way up to his house, if the town would officially re-name the street Maple Street[27-3]. 150 years later, many of those trees are still living!

*(Foote was often spelled without the final E prior to the mid-19th century, but genealogical convention is to pick one version and use it consistently—usually the modern version, which has been done in this book.)

Jonathan, his large family, and many descendants were to become leaders in the development of the town of Lee, much as the Smedleys were instrumental founding fathers in Williamstown, about 30 miles north. Ties between the two villages were close, as evidenced by a descendant of Dr. Alvan Hyde (ordained church pastor in Lee, in 1792[12-261]), who is still living in Williamstown more than 200 years later.

Like many early settlers in the Berkshires, Jonathan was a farmer, who supplemented his income by running a public house. The unique marking of his livestock was recorded as: "Jonathan foot Mark for his Creatures is a Crop of the Left Ear and a half Crop the under side the Wright Ear[12-124]."

Jonathan also did his share of civic duties, including what was then a rather important job: in Mar 1778 he was chosen as hogreeve, the official charged with enforcing regulations regarding hogs, who were let run at large under Regulation of the Law[12-12]. In 1781 he continued as hogreeve[12-20] and also was chosen as constable in 1782, a position the town council soon voted to except him from. Jonathan, Jr. was then chosen, but he refused, as did many others[12-14]. (It must have been a most unpopular job!)

In 1787, the Foote homestead briefly served as a rebel headquarters during Shays' Rebellion, when local farmers, often poorly paid former Revolutionary war soldiers, were protesting a mounting burden of new state taxes and other regulations. Spies for government interests in Stockbridge were captured at gunpoint on the property by Jonathan's daughter, Lovice, and her friend, Sarah Ellis.

The young women had dressed up as young men and, wielding *unloaded* guns, forced the intruders to dismount. When the interlopers were brought inside the house, they were revealed to be "two young bucks of Lee, and intimate acquaintances of their captors[29-159]!"

Shortly after the Footes moved to Lee, Jonathan, Jr. had married and established his own home near his parents'. In 1789, "the town voted to accept a Road leading from Jonathan Foot Junior's to Jonathan Foot Senior's" and to give them back the land the old road had been on[12-53]."

Jonathan's wife of 42 years, Sarah Fenner, who was born in Saybrook CT and was 15 years his junior, died in 1791, at age 61[19]. Less than a year later (21 Jun 1792), in the town of Tyringham, east of Lee, Jonathan was married by Rev. Joseph Avery to Temperance Holly, widow of Samuel Stanley of Great Barrington[12-316]. This second marriage was recorded in a transcript in the custody of the Town Clerk of Monterey, which in turn was copied in the back of the Town of Lee records books in 1900.

Neither Abram Foote, nor any Foote researcher who followed him, had ever noticed that Jonathan had remarried! Further proof that Temperance (Holly) Stanley had indeed become the wife of Jonathan Foote was the sale of some land in 1812, the year of her death, described as "widow Samuel Stanley (or Foot's land)." That record also noted "the widow Stanley ws [sic] the wife of Jonathon Foot....[24-210]"

At the time Jonathan re-married, the five older children were all married and presumably living nearby. His original homestead was then occupied by his son, Asahel, still unmarried at age 29, and most likely by his daughter Lovice (Lovisa), for whom the birth of two daughters was recorded, in 1789 and 1790[12-156], though no husband has ever been noted. This fact, plus her exploits during Shays' Rebellion, make her one of our more interesting ancestors!

Jonathan's youngest son, Solomon, no doubt also resided at home, until he moved to Vermont around 1795. On 24 Apr 1795 the church had voted "to give Mr. Solomon Foot, on his request, a letter of recommendation to professing christians, wherever he may be called[12-265]." Whether Jonathan and his new wife also continued to live in the house he had built in 1778 is not known.

By 1798, however, in the Massachusetts and Maine 1798 Direct Tax records[20], Jonathan Foote, Sr. is no longer listed as a property owner. By then his land holdings seemingly had been divided among his four married sons living in Lee. It appears that Asahel had inherited his father's big house, since his house-lot was valued at $300 and sat on a 1/4 acre — as opposed to $142.50 for Jonathan, Jr.'s house-lot, $104.50 for Fenner's and $142.50 for David's, (the latter three all on lots half the size of Asahel's).

Comparing the value of Asahel's house ($300) in 1798 with the house that brothers Levi and Elijah Smedley shared up in Williamstown ($977), it appears that the Smedleys were a good deal wealthier than the Footes. But many houses in Williamstown were valued at over $1,000 so it's also possible that land valuations were simply higher there.

3

This is borne out by the relative valuations of each family's farmland. The Smedleys appeared to own 353 acres, valued at $4,549.40, or $12.89/acre.

The total combined holdings of the four Foote brothers were 572.6 acres, with a value of $4713.69 or only $8.23/acre. (Obviously the quality of the acreage, a critical factor, isn't accounted for in these calculations, but the apparent greater wealth of the Smedley family may help explain why Asahel, Jr. chose to marry Mary Smedley in Williamstown after his graduation from Williams—and to remain there, rather than return with her to Lee!)

Despite Jonathan having a living, second wife when he died, he was buried in 1803 alongside his first wife, Sarah, in the Lee cemetery, right down the hill from his 1778 homestead. His grave marker has the lugubrious epitaph (typical of the period):

> *Once you must die & once for all*
> *The solemn purport weigh,*
> *For know that heaven or hell, depends*
> *On that important day[17-23].*

The epitaph of his first wife, Sarah, was even more grim:

> *Behold and see as you pass by*
> *As you are now so once was I*
> *As I am now soon you must be*
> *Prepare to die and follow me[18].*

Where the second Mrs. Jonathan Foote, Sr. (aka the Widow Stanley) wound up has not been discovered.

Asahel Foote, Sr., 1763 — 1841, Asahel, Jr.'s Father

Asahel, Sr. was the sixth of Jonathan's eight children, and like his father, was an active participant in town affairs. He was also very active in the Congregational church. He joined the church with Anna Abbot, his wife to be, on 11 Nov 1792[12-273] and was baptized that same day[12-277]. In 1793 he was a Tythingman[12-72] and in 1799 he bought a piew (sic)[12-104].

His most noteworthy accomplishment, however, was his Revolutionary War service. According to local histories, and to his son, Asahel, Jr., he

4

was serving at West Point when "the great chain[41]" was laid across the Hudson on 30 April 1778 to block British shipping[28-136]. However, the Massachusetts Soldiers and Sailors of the RevolutionaryWar[30-836] shows Asahel as having served three months and six days, in 1780, and 3 months and 12 days in 1781[30-836]. This was two years *later* than the laying of the chain. Local histories also say Asahel was 16, yet he was only 15 in April 1778, and would have been 17, a year older, in 1780.

Despite these discrepancies, the story of his miraculous trip back to Lee once he was discharged is told very consistently. In essence, upon his return in the middle of the night, his horse actually crossed the Housatonic River on a single stringer, one of the two beams that spanned the river, across which the roadbed planks were normally laid. However, the planks had been removed for repair—and as Asahel, Sr. had been sound asleep on his horse during the crossing, he only learned of his horse's incredible footwork the next morning[29-95]!

A photo of Asahel, Sr.'s tombstone from ca 1900 clearly included a Revolutionary War memorial marker[17-29], but by 2000 that marker no longer existed.

At some point after 1778 when Jonathan built the house, a tavern wing was added. Young Asahel was charged on 14 Sep 1784 in court at Great Barrington with bringing rum and other goods into the Commonwealth without paying Import and Excise taxes. One Thomas Ives on 12 Aug 1783 "did...seize one loggerhead filled with West India Rum & one six quart bottle & 1 gallon bottle containing West Indian...found by ye said Thomas on a Land Conveyance (viz) a two horse waggon belonging to & in ye possession of one Asahel Foot of Lee...." On 10 Jul 1784 it was charged that Asahel "at Egremont did import by land into the Commonweal the 100 gals of Rum, 50 gals of wine, 10 lbs of tea & divers other articles of ye value of L50...without any duty being paid upon said articles[21-679+]."

Asahel, Sr. and Anna Abbott, who was probably born in Cornwall VT, were married 21 Aug 1793 and had eight children[1]. The oldest son, Lyman, inherited the family homestead. The youngest, Asahel, Jr. was the first to go to college, an hour north (with a modern automobile) in Williamstown, where he lived almost entirely until the end of his life.

Both Asahel, Sr. and Anna were buried in the Foote family plot, just down the hill from their home. Anna's tombstone is inscribed:

> *What can avert the sting of death,*
> *And overpower the grave,*
> *Thou canst resist less heavenly faith*
> *Immortal thou canst save[17-8].*

Asahel Foote, Jr., 1804 - 1882

According to the 1871 Williams Biographical Annals[32], Asahel, Jr. had prepped at Stockbridge and Lenox Academies to prepare for Williams College, from which he graduated in 1827, at age 22[33-479].

Presumably this was quite a step up the social ladder for a farm boy, and it seems not too big a stretch of the imagination to surmise that the final E added to Foot(e) on his diploma[34] was tangible evidence of Asahel, Jr.'s social elevation. Letters to Asahel, Jr. at Williams, prior to graduation, had always addressed him as Foot, and in all previous generations in Lee, as can be seen on tombstones, Foot had also lacked a final E. By the time he graduated, however, mail was addressed to him as Asahel Foote, Jr.

Perhaps another clue to Asahel's desire to better himself was his key role in the Temperance Society at Williams[33-485]. At commencement, he even took part in a debate about *"The expediency of attempting an entire suppression of the use of ardent spirits[33-479]."*

Shedding some light on what Asahel was like as a young man are a dozen or so letters[31] to him from his first cousin, Solomon, who was a couple of years his senior at Middlebury. In the florid, flowery language of the mid-19th century, Solomon congratulates Asahel on his engagement to Mary Smedley, the 22-year-old granddaughter of one of the town's founding fathers:

> *But let us glance at a more welcome subject. What shall I say,*
> *or what shall I ask, of the unsurpassable, inimitable,*
> *unearthable, & overcomeable excellencies of the superseraphic*
> *Mary Smedley.—Human language must be infinitely*
> *insufficient to portray her virtues.—She must posses more than*
> *the united beauties of the Roxane of Aetion, the Losandra of*
> *Calamis…. Pray, forgive me Coz.*

To be a little more serious, I will say I was very much taken with
your description of her…. —let me have the transcript of a
letter or two of her's if you please…. She is the daughter of a
farmer—that is commendatory; I like a girl who is thoroughly
acquainted with the geometry of milk pans & cheese tubs; &
well versed in the mechanics of the shuttle & the quill wheel.

What makes this rather silly (by today's standards) letter most amazing is
that the young Solomon Foot who penned it on 27 Feb 1828 went on to
be a US Senator from VT from 1851 until his death in 1866—and was
President Pro Tem of the Senate throughout most of the Civil War. (That
made him #3 in line behind the VP and Speaker of the House should
anything happen to Pres. Lincoln!)[1-113].

A few months after Solomon's congratulatory (or was it?) letter, Asahel
had his "Intentions" to marry Mary published in Lee[19-131]—like the
posting of banns in England.

If you consider Mary's situation at the time, it was not only fortuitous for
Asahel to marry the daughter of a leading citizen. It was also a way for
Mary to escape spinsterhood and getting stuck caring for the old folks
living at home. All of her siblings, even a younger sister, were already
married, with her sisters presumably living elsewhere—so no doubt that
would have been Mary's lot.

Yet a couple of later letters suggest that Mary may not have been such a
great catch, apart from her social and financial status. Her daughter-in-
law—who was legendary as a fine, upstanding Christian lady—had little
use for Mary. In fact, she made this abundantly clear in a letter dated 21
April 1895 to her daughter, who was away at Smith College[3-227]:

> *Your grandma Foote [Mary Smedley] was so excessively*
> *narrow in her sympathies, so 'exclusive' they used to say, that*
> *she was positively of no earthly use to her day and generation.*
> *Not a person in Williamstown could ever say 'I am better and*
> *happier for Mrs. Foote's being here!'… This is not my*
> *opinion, it is a well-recognized fact. She simply could not or*
> *would not open her heart to take anyone in, and she trained*
> *her children so….[3-227]*

From an 1862 letter[10] sent by Mary's son-in-law (a doctor with the 15th
Ohio Infantry during the Civil War) to his wife, Hattie, who was staying

with her family in Williamstown, we learn that Mary was suffering seriously from asthma. The letter suggests a couple of treatments:

As regards your mother's case - Let her get some of the extr. of Stramonium, dilute it sufficiently with water…then saturate some sheets of soft paper…dry them thoroughly & then…<u>burn</u> pieces of the prepared paper <u>inhaling</u> the smoke until slight nausea or vertigo is produced. Or…let her try inhaling cautiously a little Chloroform….

A quick Google search indicates these chemicals are quite lethal! Even more suggestive, the librarian who cataloged the letter for the University of Michigan's Civil War archives, knowing nothing at all about Mary Smedley Foote, nonetheless speculated:

…his recommendation of chloroform to aid his mother-in-law's asthma may or may not have other overtones!

The 17 Feb 1828 letter above from Solomon Foote was addressed to Asahel in New Ipswich NH as "Principal" of Appleton Academy. Presumably Mary joined him there after their marriage on 14 Aug 1828[2]. With not very many career paths available in those days, both Asahel and Solomon had begun post-graduate life as teachers.

Sometime before the 1830 census, Asahel and Mary had moved to St. Albans VT, about 40 miles north of Hinesburg (where Mary's uncles Moses and Elisha resided[25]). An advertisement[35] "For the Quarter ending August 17th, 1830" lists Asahel as "Superintendent for Gentlemen" at the Franklin County Grammar School in St. Albans, where their first child was born on 8 Sep 1830[25].

Within a few years, however, Asahel developed ambitions to start his own school, in Mary's old home in Williamstown. By 1833, Asahel had obtained recommendations for his school from locally prominent men such as Alvan Hyde, minister and leading citizen of Lee, and E. D. Griffin, President of Williams when Asahel had been a student there[35].

An 1838 ad[35] for the boarding school ("Mr. Foote's Seminary for Boys") included a recommendation from Mark Hopkins, the then-president of Williams. The ad claimed the school had been in "successful operation" for the last five years, with two terms per year: mid-May to mid-November, and mid-November to mid-May. A 4-week vacation was included between each term.

The post and beam house that Mary's father built sometime between 1810 and 1820 (based on census records), could well have proved too small to house many student boarders, along with Mary's parents, Mary and Asahel, and their growing brood of children. So presumably the brick addition to the house (most likely built with bricks from a clay pit on the property[14-10]) was constructed around the time the school was established. Around the same time, Mary's father, Elisha, sold the entire property to his son-in-law, Asahel—for $2000 in 1835 according to one local researcher[8].

Asahel, however, seemed as drawn to horticulture as he was to education. Perhaps it was for men like him that the term "gentleman farmer" was coined. Certainly, that is what Asahel soon became. As early as 1835, with his school just getting off the ground, Asahel sketched a plan of an orchard on the back of a letter from the father of a student[35].

His interest in fruit trees was scarcely unexpected, having grown up surrounded by his grandfather's orchards in Lee. Now that he was living among the orchards of his wife's family (supposedly the Smedleys were the first settlers in Williamstown to start cultivating fruits[28-669]), he was certainly no stranger to their propagation.

When unspecified ill heath[11-203] forced Asahel to give up the 24/7 rigors of running a boarding school, he naturally turned to agriculture, and the propagation of fruits, in particular. The first entry he made in his "Farmer's Journal[37]," on 1 Jan 1841, referred to that year as "the first year of my agricultural life....[37]"

As an educated, Renaissance man, he not only developed superlative fruit varieties, he also experimented with new agricultural techniques, and wrote about them. His "Essay on the Manufacture of Manures" is still listed on Amazon, and won him at least two prizes, one for $50 in 1843[35] (about $1,600 in 2015 dollars). It began with a quotation:

> *A good agriculturalist will neglect no means of forming dung-heaps: it ought to be his first, and daily care, for without dung there is no harvest. —Chaptal*

Asahel also won a $20 "Premium" in 1866 from the Berkshire Agricultural Society for his "System of Farm Accounts[37]" (of which his "Farmer's Journal" is scarcely a good example!)

Another example of Asahel as both scholar and farmer is his 20-page lecture on the Profits of Agriculture[35]:

> *I observe then, in the first place, that agriculture is profitable, in that it furnishes to the farmer a rational, dignified and honorable occupation.*

Asahel was also a savvy businessman, however, who made full use of the advertising media available at the time. He employed newspaper ads, like the following from 1852, which reads:

> *FRUIT TREES.*
> *NEW CATALOGUES of the Greylock Nurseries may be had gratis, by calling at S. REED & CO's Agricultural Store, in this village [Pittsfield], or by applying (postage paid) to the subscriber at Williamstown. ASAHEL FOOTE, Proprietor. P.S. An extra lot of Bartlett, Seckle and Virgaloo Pear Trees for sale as above[35].*

He also handed out broadsides, a very popular advertising medium of the day. One dated March, 1852 was headed: "At the Greylock Nurseries, in Williamstown, Mass., are propagated the following varieties of fruit trees, most of which are ready for sale the present season[35]." Then listed are summer, fall and winter apples and pears, plus plums and cherries (light and dark colored), as well as quinces, native grapes, gooseberries and currants. 131 varieties of winter apples alone are included!

Apple trees cost 20 cts and were "packed in the securest manner" (the purchaser was billed for the packing) and delivered to the train station in North Adams, where presumably they were shipped C.O.D. to the purchaser. Customers were assured that the new grading system of the American Pomological Congress would be employed, and any stock falling below the grade of Very Good would be rejected from future Nursery Lists.

Perhaps the best advertising for Asahel Foote's fruit trees was his reputation. Many of his varieties of apples, pears and other fruits appear in a 19th century horticultural "bible," known as The fruits and fruit-trees of America; or, the culture, propagation, and management, in the garden and orchard, of fruit-trees generally; with descriptions of all the finest varies of fruit, native and foreign, cultivated in this country, by A.J. Downing,…second revision and correction, with large additions, by Charles Downing. New York: John Wiley & Son,…1869[35]. Asahel Foote's own copy is inscribed "Hon. Asahel Foote with the compliments of his friend Chas. Downing."

At some point in its history, the property where Mary had grown up, and Asahel had had his school and his nursery business, became known as the Orchards. Even the upscale hotel that was built on the land in 1984 continued to be called the Orchards, with ads for the new hotel appearing in the *New Yorker*[8]. (The hotel had been preceded by a typical 1950s motel, complete with little cabins—and a swimming pool!)

Fortunately for preservationists, when the land was cleared for the new hotel, the original house and its addition were saved from the wrecking ball by being moved around the corner to 62 Stratton Road. The firm that moved the old building said it was the heaviest house they had ever moved—as the walls in the addition had been made of solid brick[8]! As for the orchards themselves, they have all been uprooted or plowed under, sad to say.

Not long after being relocated, the former Orchards house was reported to be haunted. At the time, it was serving as an office building and the custodian, along with several employees, reported everything from creaking stairways and banging doors to maniacal laughter ringing loudly in the night, according to an article in the *Advocate* of 24 January 1990[8].

During Asahel's life in this house, he not only ran a successful prep school and developed a national reputation as an orchardist, he also led an exemplary life as a generous and active citizen. Some of his many contributions include:

- On 10 Jun 1842, he provided more than an acre of his property adjacent to the Green River for the town's first burial ground, known today as East Lawn Cemetery. (According to his "Farmer's Journal," he received $300 for this donation[37].)

- Also in 1842 he gave $100 for rebuilding part of Williams College after a tragic fire, and another $400 to rebuild the Meeting House which burned down on 20 Jan 1866[37].

- He served as President of the Board of County Commissioners, and in 1844 was also elected to the State Senate[32].

- In 1855 he was chosen with two others to find the exact spot at Lake George where Col. Ephraim Williams was slain in the French and Indian War—so that a monument could be erected there[37].

- In 1859, Asahel was a founder and one of three vice presidents of the Hoosac Valley Agricultural Society[28-413], in addition to his earlier leadership role with both the Berkshire Horticultural Society and the Berkshire Agricultural Society[37].

- In some ways most important, Asahel was chosen on 12 Sep1838 as a Deacon of the Congregational Church, an honorary title that was used with his name for the rest of his life[35].

As mentioned earlier, Asahel was truly a gentleman farmer—and renaissance man—as demonstrated by the language and imagery in this report by Asahel and other committee members about a local ploughing contest.

Report of the Committee on the Ploughing Match, **Pittsfield Sun**, *15 Oct 1846, p 2:*

...the unprecedented concourse of spectators—the inspiriting presence of so many of the beautiful daughters, that came to smile upon the virtuous sons of Old Berkshire, as they vied with each other in wielding the most important implement that art has ever yet constructed...the joyous alacrity and skillful dexterity of the ploughman...the unretarded progress of the stately plough, winning its way through the surface of the earth, like the noble ship through the surface of the waters[35]....

Ploughing was hardly relegated to blue-collar labor in Asahel's view!

Asahel also served his community in more intellectual ways. He was part of a Committee of Examination at Maplewood Young Ladies Institute in Pittsfield, which described the school as excellent in the report published in the 9 Feb 1858 *Berkshire County Eagle*:

The advantages here enjoyed for the attainment of elegant accomplishments, solid knowledge, and christian graces are such, that wise and true parents might well rejoice in the privilege of entrusting their daughters to the influences which preside at the beautiful Maplewood[35].

Coincidently, it is highly likely that Asahel's future daughter-in-law, Sarah Cole (who was known to have attended Maplewood[3-222], and who would have been 16 in 1858) was in attendance that day.

An even greater coincidence is that fourteen years later, Sarah proved to be the proverbial "girl next door," becoming the wife of Asahel's son, Charles Rollin[3-223]. Sarah, daughter of Harvey Towner Cole, grew up in a house just to the west of the Foote property, next to her father's big brick general store on Water Street[3-6]. (Both buildings are still standing today, though the house was moved a long time ago, around the corner to Grundy Court.)

Just a few years after Charles Rollin's and Sarah' marriage, toward the end of Asahel's life, he seemingly donated his personal collection of agricultural books to a public library that was established in a corner of the Cole store in 1874. Fittingly, the librarian was Asahel's son—and Harvey's son-in-law—Charles Rollin Foote[11-244].

Of Asahel's domestic life, and of his wife, Mary, we know much less, unfortunately. In the late 19th century, women, like children, were still mostly seen and not heard; their contributions to society, in the form of domestic arts, largely went unrecognized in any public record.

Even something that today would be considered the province of the housewife—a compilation of traditional family recipes to pass on to future generations—was created by Asahel. The small, hand-bound booklet he produced contains recipes (called receipts in those days) for all manner of stews, puddings, baked goods—and even medicinal potions, like brandy and salt for indigestion[35].

Only one photograph of the family, dated around 1856, has survived. At that time, Harriet, the eldest, had already married and was no longer living at home[1]. The other four children were, presumably, between 22 and 15 in the photo. The only boy is Charles Rollin, who would graduate from Williams in 1859[3-223]. From letters[10], it is clear that daughters Harriet and Mary attended boarding school, and in Asahel's "Farmer's Journal," there are many notations of tuition being sent to various parts of the country for all four girls. Education was evidently a life-long priority of Asahel Foote (and his descendants)!

More details about the adult lives of Asahel's and Mary's daughters are summarized in the Foote Ancestor Register Report (FARR) at the back of this book, while Charles Rollin is described at some length in George Clapp's book about Charles Rollin's wife, Sarah Caroline Cole[3].

Despite the lack of family letters and photos, Asahel's "Farmer's Journal" presents indirectly a wonderful portrait of the Foote family's domestic life. This 137-page notebook, in which Asahel meticulously recorded every nickel he spent or earned between 1841 and 1868, is an absolute goldmine of first-hand biographical information. Fortunately, it was preserved for posterity; unfortunately, it resides on the west coast (at the prestigious Huntington Library in Pasadena) and not on the east coast, where all the events that were recorded took place.

The stated purpose of the journal was to record "...my labors and their results, together with all such matters as might be worth reviewing or referring to, at any future time[37]." Indeed, the bulk of the entries enumerate crops being planted and harvested, livestock being bred, shorn, skinned and butchered, eggs, butter, hay, wood, honey, potatoes and numerous fruits and vegetables being sold, repairs being made, supplies and farm equipment being purchased—and an almost daily weather report.

Record-breaking temperatures of 32 below zero were noted with exclamation points, along with a comparison of the freezing conditions from as far away as St. Louis and New York City. Frosts as late as May 30 and as early as the end of August were heralded. Never-ending snowfalls between November 1844 and March 1845 were rejoiced at, since they enabled goods to be transported by sleigh—much the cheapest and easiest method—all winter long. To a farmer, nothing was as vital as the weather!

Not just the business side of country living was noted by Asahel. The arrival in spring of swallows and orioles, and peeping frogs, was remarked upon, as well as the tragic death of a flock of sheep that was killed by lightening under a buttonwood tree. The intense efforts expended to save a sick horse were described in detail. Many animals were given names, even though they were destined for the slaughterhouse. When a white oak was felled, its rings were carefully counted—dating the tree to 1641!

Since travel costs were duly recorded, a vivid picture emerges of how amazingly well travelled the Foote family was, given their remote location in the Berkshires, and the challenges of travel in the mid-nineteenth century. Between business trips of Asahel and Charles, and schooling and teaching assignments for all four girls (including Mt. Holyoke in 1847 for Harriet, the eldest daughter), family members visited Albany, Rochester, Brooklyn and Saratoga NY; Pittsfield, Lee, Great Barrington, Lenox, Charlemont, Springfield, Newton, Boston and Worcester MA; Hartford and New Haven CT and as far away as Covington KY and New Orleans—for which Asahel saw Harriet set sail (at age 20) from New York City on 22 Dec 1850. Even Asahel's wife appears to have travelled by herself to Ohio in 1854.

Other domestic entries included a long list of charities and investments. Donations included the Bible Society, the Seaman's Friend's Society, the Colonization Society and the Female Benevolent Society, while occasional bonds were bought in local railroad ventures, the U S government, and the "Midas Mining Company."

While the life of a farmer—even an educated one, with specialized skills as a horticulturalist—was very basic, the Footes' life appears quite refined in many ways. Not only was $4,000 spent on a piano, which was frequently tuned, at least some of the children had singing lessons, and their sheet music was collected in bound volumes. Many books and magazines were purchased, such as *Scientific American, Mother's Magazine, Youth's Companion, NY Observer, Tri-Weekly Republican*, along with various political and religious tracts. Asahel bought a copy of Nathaniel Goodwin's genealogy, The Foote Family, published in 1849, so he would have been well aware of the prestigious history of his family.

In 1846, two portraits of Mary were painted, and pictures were occasionally framed, including one of Asahel's highly respected cousin,

Solomon Foote (who served as President Pro Tem of the Senate during the Civil War). Other household luxuries included wallpaper, furs and fine fabrics for clothes, and a $45 gold watch!

One unusual purchase on 17 Aug 1865 was a "1/2 pint of Rum!!!" (The exclamation points were included in Asahel's journal entry). As he had renewed his membership in the Temperance Society that March (consistent with his belief in abstinence first noted in a college graduation day debate), it must be assumed the rum was for culinary or medicinal purposes. Indeed, most illnesses were treated with home remedies. Only rarely was an expenditure noted for a visit to a doctor or dentist, or for a specialty item such as spectacles for Mary and a glass eye for Charles Rollin.

Asahel also included a few historical events of particular importance to him. Along with a complete tally of the 1842 Massachusetts election (in which he was elected to the Massachusetts State Legislature), he highlighted (with a sketch of a pointing finger) the1865 Centennial of the founding of Williamstown. Yet, not a mention was made of the Civil War—even though his eldest daughter and a grandchild were living with the family in Williamstown while his son-in-law served as a surgeon with the Ohio Infantry. He also noted the death of his cousin, Solomon, soon after the Civil War, with no mention at all of Solomon's prominent role in government during the war.

Given that the "Farmer's Journal" was primarily an income and expense ledger, it is still noteworthy that Asahel included so few records of important family events. One that did take his fancy, however, was the exploration of South America by his son-in-law, James Orton (a former boarder who had married his daughter, Ellen—and who later became a colleague of Charles Darwin and a noted naturalist in his own right.) In 1867, Asahel noted the entire itinerary of Orton's 10,048-mile trip. (In 1877, on a subsequent trip, Orton died on Lake Titicaca, where a memorial was erected by Vassar College in 1921. Orton's daughter, Anna, then aged 59, travelled to the ceremony all the way from her California home.)

The picture that Asahel's "Farmer's Journal" paints of one of Williamstown's most successful citizens, gives rise to a basic question. *Why*, in the spring of 1879, at age 74, did he make the strenuous trip west to Pasadena CA "which in 1880 numbered 391 souls[3-10]? " And why did his two unmarried, 40-ish daughters also relocate nearly 3,000 miles from home—along with his married son, whose wife and four-year old daughter followed just a few months later[3-223]?

One reason probably was that both his wife and eldest daughter Hattie had died in 1876—so he had no spouse or grandchildren to keep him in Williamstown.

The main reason, however, for uprooting this prominent branch of the Foote/Smedley clan was most likely son Charles Rollin's determination to "GO WEST!" This dream apparently was eloquently expressed in a now-missing letter dating back to his college days, 20 years earlier. In pursuit of this goal, in April of 1865, Charles had already traveled to West Virginia, and a year later to Grand Rapids (Michigan, presumably[37]).

Pasadena, in particular, was widely known as a western "paradise," with the names of settlers from both the Northeast and Midwest—as well as from England—predominating in early city directories[4-129]. So this was the family's ultimate choice.

A couple of years before he went to California, Asahel was invited to speak at a Lee Centennial Celebration in 1877. He couldn't attend, because of ill health—and his need to install a new irrigation system— but instead he wrote the committee a very long and charming letter. After several pages of detailed childhood recollections, he concluded with gentle self-deprecation:

> *Here, I 'guess' I will 'haul up'. When I penned the first sentence in this communication, my simple purpose was to acknowledge the receipt of your very kind letter, and acquaint you with the reasons of my non-appearance at your Centennial; but my thoughts posted off in the direction which you see they have taken, and I just let them run—'at random,' I fear you will be tempted to add*[29-97].

When Asahel arrived in Pasadena, he purchased in June 1879 twenty acres of what would later be among the most prime property in town[3-223]. His land on Orange Grove Avenue overlooked the Arroyo Seco, a north-south trail created by southern California's earliest indigenous inhabitants, which was used by each successive group of settlers from Spain, Mexico and the eastern United States[23].

There he built a large house for his unmarried daughters. With no father, brother nor husbands to take care of them back in Williamstown, it was their fate to move west, under the protection of their brother, who would soon be the only existing male member of their immediate family.

In 1882, Asahel returned to Williamstown, where he became ill and died on 15 July 1882[3-224]. His daughters soon sold the Orchards property, remaining permanently in southern California[22-104]. They also sold Asahel's original Pasadena house to their neighbor, Mrs. Bangs[16-2], and moved further south[22-104].

Under the proprietorship of Mrs. Bangs, Asahel's magnificent home (which boasted the first hardwood floors in Pasadena and overlooked the scenic Arroyo Seco), became a popular boarding house. It was later incorporated into the enormous Vista del Arroyo Hotel—with its mahogany handrail surviving both transitions[16-2]! During WWII the government acquired the property, and the oldest section of the hotel became part of the Army's McCornack General Hospital. That facility now serves as a Court of Appeals and Federal Building[38].

As for Asahel, his obituary in the 20 Jul 1882 Adams Transcript sums up his life very eloquently:

> *The death of Mr. Foote removes one of the old Williamstown residents and Williams College graduates, the record of whose life has from its earliest days been connected with Williamstown history and public spirit. Earnest interest in Williamstown, its business and social progress and the condition of its college was a prominent characteristic of the deceased and in his earlier years much of his labor was spent in public work and enterprise....[39]*

In brief, in just over 50 years, Asahel Foote had arrived at Williams as a simple farm boy, added an e to his name and married into the prominent Smedley family, become a leading citizen in his own right—only to have his offspring leave behind everything he had achieved, to begin a new life on the other side of the continent. Instead of apple orchards, the family was invested in orange groves!

Comparing a photo of son Charles Rollin's first house in Pasadena with the Orchards in Williamstown, it's hard not to wonder if the decision to go west was ever regretted. But, that is another story—to be told someday, it is hoped, by someone in the next generation.

END NOTE: THE *OTHER* ASAHEL FOOTE

The story of Asahel Foote in Williamstown would not be complete without noting there was a second Asahel Foot and family living in town. Not only did this present research complications, it also created an enormous puzzle when it became clear that the second Asahel was an illiterate "negro" (as Vital Records of the 19th century labeled people of color), born in NY, and 25 years older than "our" Asahel.

Even in the mid-19th century, the name Asahel was not very common, nor was Foot. The odds are incredibly small that there could be two adult males with that name—yet with no relationship to each other—in a town with a total population of only 2,626 people (in 1850)[25]. Yet extensive research has produced no evidence of the slightest connection.

An early 20th century Williams College mathematics professor, Elmer I. Shepard, took it upon himself to collect information on some 50,000 western Massachusetts families, compiling all his findings on file cards for each family[40]. This pulled together data from local Vital Records, Federal and State Censuses and other sources that can no longer be found. So at least we do know the negro Asahel had two wives who died, and at least five children. The cause of death of one child was "drunkenness of parents," though no records have been found of any punishment of the parents, nor does this Asahel appear in a bad light in any other way.

On the contrary, in boyhood reminiscences published in 1895, one Williamstown resident tells the following tale:

> *An old colored man by the name of Asahel Foot (one of the freed New York slaves claimed to have been one of the old Patroon servants) used to work for the Whitmans and the good women used to instruct Asahel and talk to him much on religious subjects, and Asahel thought himself good and sure for the kingdom, having been taught there was no distinction in color there and that all were equal. Asahel came into the house one cold winter morning when Mrs. Whitman said: "It is very cold, Asahel." "Very" said Asahel, "but, Mrs. Whitman, we have only a few more days here below, and we shall find it very different when we are walking the streets of the new Jerusalem arm in arm together there[22-93]."*

FOOTE ANCESTOR REGISTER REPORT (FARR)

Seven generations of birth, marriage and death data, beginning with the 1st generation in America, along with some biographical information.

First Generation

----

1. Nathaniel FOOTE[13] was born on 21 Sep 1592 in Colchester, Essex, England. Nathaniel died in Wethersfield, Hartford CT, on 20 Dec 1644; he was 52. He was the first of his Foote line to settle in America. In ca 1615 when Nathaniel was 22, he married **Elizabeth DEMING**[13] in England. She was born ca 1595 in Colchester, Essex England, and died in Wethersfield, Hartford CT, on 28 Jul 1683; she was 88. Elizabeth was buried in Wethersfield, Hartford CT. She had married 2nd Governor Thomas Welles, Sr. in 1646.

According to Abram Foote in 1907, "From all that we can learn Mr. Foote came from Shalford, in Colchester, England, and settled in Watertown, Massachusetts. The first mention I find made of his name is in the Records of the Colony of Massachusetts Bay, in 1633, when he took the oath of freeman.... Whether Mr. Foote was among the pioneers from Watertown, who made the first lodgment in, or before, 1635, on the banks of the Connecticut at Pyquag (Wethersfield CT), is not known, but his name is found in its first Records, and among those to whom the first distribution of land was made; and he, therefore, must have shared in all the dangers and privation of that long and toilsome journey through the wilderness in 1636, and have encountered all the horrors and trials of the first winter in their new home.... In the original distribution of the lands of the town, as recorded in 1640, Mr. Foote had assigned him a house lot of ten acres on the east side of Broad Street, near the south end of the street.... Mr. Foote became the owner of several other tracts of land, laying partly in the Great Meadows east of his house lot, and containing in the whole, upwards of four hundred acres. The cultivation of his land constituted his main business, although he was called by his neighbors to participate in the public trust of the town, and in 1644 was appointed a delegate to the General Court[1]."

20

Nathaniel and Elizabeth had the following children:

   i. Elizabeth[13]. Born on 8 Sep 1616 in Colchester, Essex England. Elizabeth died in Wethersfield, Hartford CT, on 8 Sep 1700; she was 84.
      In 1638 when Elizabeth was 21, she married **Josiah CHURCHILL**[13] in Wethersfield, Hartford. Born ca 1615. Josiah died in Wethersfield, Hartford CT, on 1 Jan 1686; he was 71.

2 ii. Nathaniel Jr. (ca 1619/20-Jun 1655)

   iii. Mary[13]. Born ca 1623 in England. Mary died in Wethersfield, Hartford CT, aft Aug 1685; she was 62.
      In 1642 when Mary was 19, she first married **John STODDARD Sr.**[13] in Wethersfield, Hartford CT. Born in 1620 in England. John died in Wethersfield, Hartford CT, in Dec 1664; he was 44.
      On 4 Apr 1674 when Mary was 51, she second married **John GOODRICH Jr.**[13] in Wethersfield, Hartford CT. Born ca 1616 in St. James, Bury St. Edmunds, Suffolk, England. John died in Wethersfield, Hartford CT, in Apr 1680; he was 64.
      In 1683 when Mary was 60, she third married **Lieutenant Thomas TRACY**[13]. Born ca 1610. Thomas died on 7 Nov 1685; he was 75.

   iv. Lieutenant Robert[13]. Born on 8 Dec 1627 in England. Robert died in Branford, New Haven CT, in 1681; he was 53.
      On 6 Aug 1659 when Robert was 31, he married **Sarah POTTER**[13] in Wethersfield, Hartford CT. Born ca 1639. Sarah died in Branford, New Haven CT, on 22 Aug 1706; she was 67.

   v. Frances[13]. Born in 1629 in East Bergholst, Suffolk, England.
      In 1648 when Frances was 19, she first married **Sergeant John DICKINSON**[13] in Wethersfield, Hartford CT. John died on 19 May 1676.

On 21 Aug 1677 when Frances was 48, she second married **Francis BARNARD**[13] in Hadley, Hampshire CT. Born ca 1617. Francis died in Hadley, Hampshire CT, on 3 Feb 1698; he was 81.

vi.   Sarah[13]. Born ca 1632 in England. Sarah died in Stratford, Fairfield CT, in 1673, at age 41. In 1652 when Sarah was 20, she married **Sergeant Jeremiah JUDSON Sr.**[13] in Wethersfield, Hartford CT. Born ca 1621 in England. Jeremiah died in Stratford, Fairfield CT, on 15 May 1700; he was 79.

vii.   Rebecca[13]. Born on 3 Sep 1634 in England. Rebecca died in Hadley, Hampshire MA, on 6 Apr 1701; she was 66.
In 1657 when Rebecca was 22, she first married **Lieutenant Philip SMITH Sr.**[13], son of SMITH, in Wethersfield, Hartford CT. Born ca 1633 in England. Philip died on 19 Jan 1685; he was 52.
On 2 Oct 1688 when Rebecca was 54, she second married **Major Aaron COOK**[13]. Born in 1610. Aaron died 5 Sep 1690; he was 80.

Second Generation

---

2. Nathaniel FOOTE Jr.[13] was born ca 1619/20 in Colchester, Essex, England. He was baptized 5 Mar 1619/1620.
Nathaniel died in Hadley, Hampshire MA, in Jun 1655; he was 36. In 1646 when Nathaniel was 27, he married **Elizabeth SMITH**[13], daughter of Lieutenant Samuel SMITH Sr. & Elizabeth ?, in Wethersfield, Hartford CT. She was born ca 1627 in England, and died aft 5 Jan 1701/2; she was 74.

They had the following children:

3   i.   Nathaniel III (10 Jan 1647/48-12 Jan 1702/03).

ii.   Samuel Foote Sr.[13] Born on 1 May 1649 in Wethersfield, Hartford CT. Samuel Foote died on 7 Sep 1689; he was 40.

22

Ca 1670 when Samuel Foote was 20, he married **Mary MERRICK**[13] in Springfield, Hampden MA. Born ca 1650.

iii.   Daniel Sr.[13] Born in 1652 in Wethersfield, Hartford CT.

Ca 1679 when Daniel was 27, he first married **Sarah ?**[13]. Born ca 1658, Sarah died in Stratford, Fairfield CT, on 26 Mar 1704; she was 46.

Ca 1710 when Daniel was 58, he second married **Mary ?**[13].

iv.   Elizabeth[13]. Born in 1654 in Wethersfield, Hartford CT. Elizabeth died in Deerfield, Franklin CT, on 16 Sep 1696; she was 42. She was killed by Indians along with 3 of her children.

On 10 Nov 1670 when Elizabeth was 16, she married **Daniel BELDEN Sr.**[13], son of William BELDEN & Thomasin ?, in Wethersfield, Hartford CT. Born on 30 Nov 1648 in Wethersfield, Hartford CT, Daniel died in Deerfield, Franklin CT, on 14 Aug 1732; he was 83.

Third Generation

----

3. Nathaniel FOOTE III[13] was born on 10 Jan 1647/48 in Wethersfield, Hartford CT. Nathaniel died in Wethersfield, Hartford CT, on 12 Jan 1702/03; he was 55. On 2 May 1672 when Nathaniel was 25, he married **Margaret BLISS**[13], daughter of Nathaniel BLISS, in Springfield, Hampden MA. Born ca 1650, Margaret died in Colchester, New London CT, on 3 Apr 1745; she was 95.

According to Abram Foote in 1907, "After residing in Hatfield two years, he removed to Springfield, like every householder, he was called into the service of his country against the Indians, and was actively engaged in the bloody and successful attack on their encampment at the falls in the Connecticut River a few miles above Deerfield, since called Turners's Falls…. From Springfield, Mr. Foote removed to Stratford, where his house lot of one acre was on Main Street…. This lot he conveyed in March 1680 to Benjamin Lewis, having decided to move with his family to Branford, where, in February 1679, he was admitted as a planter of the town, and a home lot was granted to him 'on the condition that it should have a tenantable house built upon it within two years, and that he come to settle amongst us, or else the lot to return to the town again.' In pursing his manifest destiny to migrate, Mr. Foote conveyed his lot with sundry other lots to which had become possessed, to Jonathan Pitman, of Stratford, and moved to Wethersfield, where he continued to reside till his death, although he had, previous to that event, planned another removal to a new settlement begun under his enterprise, a Jeremy's Farm, since and now called Colchester.... This land was conveyed by Owaneco, Sachem of Monhegan, for the consideration of love and affection to Nathaniel Foote, to be distributed by him according to his discretion, except for fifty acres to be selected by himself, which he had the privilege of reserving to himself and his heirs forever. The settlement was commenced in 1701, but on account of failing health, Mr. Foote did not remove.... His widow and four youngest children... subsequently moved to Colchester.... Nathaniel was mainly a house carpenter but also practiced as an attorney in the colonial courts[1]."

Nathaniel and Margaret had the following children:

      i.   Sarah[13]. Born on 25 Feb 1672/73 in Hatfield, Hampshire MA. Sarah died on 24 Jul 1756; she was 84.
              On 30 Nov 1691 when Sarah was 19, she married **Thomas OLCOTT**[13] in Wethersfield, Hartford CT. Born ca 1670.

      ii.   Margaret[13]. Born on 1 Dec 1674 in Hatfield, Hampshire MA.

      iii.   Elizabeth[13]. Born on 23 Jun 1677 in Wethersfield, Hartford CT.
              In Jun 1701 when Elizabeth was 23, she married **Robert TURNER**[13] in Wethersfield, Hartford CT. Born ca 1675. Robert died ca 1745; he was 70.

      iv.   Mary[13]. Born on 24 Nov 1679 in Wethersfield, Hartford CT.
              On 14 May 1706 when Mary was 26, she married **Daniel ROSE Jr.**[13] in Wethersfield, Hartford CT. Born on 20 Aug 1667 in Wethersfield, Hartford CT.

v.   Nathaniel IV[13]. Born on 9 Sep 1682 in Wethersfield, Hartford CT. Nathaniel died in Colchester, New London CT, on 20 Aug 1774; he was 91.

On 4 Jul 1711 when Nathaniel was 28, he first married **Ann CLARK**[13] in Colchester, New London CT. Born ca 1682. Ann died in Colchester, New London CT, on 25 Jun 1726; she was 44.

On 13 Sep 1727 when Nathaniel was 45, he second married **Mary ?**[13] in Colchester, New London CT. Born ca 1685.

vi.   Ephraim Sr.[13] Born on 13 Feb 1685 in Wethersfield, Hartford CT. Ephraim died in Colchester, New London CT, on 10 Jun 1765; he was 80.

In Jun 1708 when Ephraim was 23, he married **Sarah CHAMBERLAIN**[13] in Colchester, New London CT. Born 10 Mar 1693. Sarah died 9 Jun 1777; she was 84.

4   vii.   Josiah Sr. (27 Sep 1688-Dec 1778)

viii.   Joseph[13]. Born on 28 Dec 1690 in Wethersfield, Hartford CT.

On 12 Dec 1719 when Joseph was 28, he first married **Ann CLOTHIER**[13] in Colchester, New London CT. Born ca 1695. Ann died on 15 Apr 1740; she was 45.

On 2 Sep 1740 when Joseph was 49, he second married **Hannah POMEROY**[13]. Born ca 1698.

ix.   Eunice[13]. Born on 10 May 1694 in Wethersfield, Hartford CT.

On 3 Dec 1712 when Eunice was 18, she married **Michael TAINTOR Jr.**[13] in Colchester, New London CT. Born on 6 Sep 1680. Michael died 11 Mar 1771; he was 90.

4. Josiah FOOTE Sr.[13] was born on 27 Sep 1688 in Wethersfield, Hartford CT. Josiah died in Dec 1778 in Colchester CT, aged 90. On 7 Dec 1712 when Josiah was 24, he married **Sarah WELLS**[13], daughter of Noah WELLS Sr. & Mary WHITE. Born on 30 Oct 1692 in Hadley, Hampshire MA, Sarah died on 3 Aug 1766; she was 73.

They had the following children:

	i.	Josiah Jr.[13] Born on 28 Jul 1713 in Colchester, New London CT. Josiah died in Windsor CT, on 17 Feb 1798; he was 84. On 7 Dec 1738 when Josiah was 25, he married **Sarah CHAMBERLAIN**[13], daughter of William CHAMBERLAIN, in Colchester, New London CT. Born in 1718 in Colchester, New London CT, Sarah died in Windsor CT, on 29 Dec 1799; she was 81.
5	ii.	Jonathan (23 Mar 1715-11 Nov 1803)
	iii.	Eunice[13]. Born on 26 Sep 1716 in Colchester, New London CT. Eunice died on 22 Oct 1801; she was 85. On 13 May 1735 when Eunice was 18, she married **Josiah TREADWAY Sr.**[13] in Colchester, New London CT. Josiah died on 16 May 1790.
	iv.	David[13]. Born on 24 Feb 1718. David died on 3 Sep 1757; he was 39. Unmarried.
	v.	Joseph[13]. Born on 12 May 1721 in Colchester, New London CT. Joseph died in Feb 1757; he was 35. Joseph married **Thankful PEASE**[13].
	vi.	Habbakah[13]. Born on 27 Jan 1722/23 in Colchester, New London CT. Habbakah died in 1803; he was 80. Habbakah married **Mary (Chamberlain) WELLES**[13], daughter of William CHAMBERLAIN. Born ca 1721 in Colchester, New London CT. Mary (Chamberlain) died on 14 May 1801; she was 80.

vii	Mary[13]. Born on 22 May 1726 in Colchester, New London CT. Mary died on 19 Jun 1811; she was 85.

Mary[13]. Born on 22 May 1726 in Colchester, New London CT. Mary died on 19 Jun 1811; she was 85.
On 10 Oct 1748 when Mary was 22, she married **Jonas WILDE**[13] in Colchester, New London CT. Jonas died on 4 May 1802.

viii. John[13]. Born on 15 Aug 1728 in Colchester, New London CT. John died in Hebron CT, on 9 Oct 1818; he was 90.
John first married **Anna THOMPSON**[13], daughter of John THOMPSON & Mary OTIS on 18 Apr 1768. She was born in 1734. Anna died on 28 Mar 1798; she was 64.
John second married in 1799 **Maria Cathrine MILLER**[13], daughter of John MILLER. Born in 1759. Maria Cathrine died in Glastonbury CT, on 5 Nov 1845; she was 86.

ix. Sarah[13]. Born on 28 Jan 1730/31 in Colchester, New London CT. Sarah died on 15 Aug 1818; she was 88.
On 5 Jan 1758 when Sarah was 27, she married **Cullick ELY Sr.**[13], son of Richard ELY & Margaret OLCOTT, in Lyme, New London CT. Born in Jan 1733. Cullick died on 29 Aug 1821; he was 88.

x. Catherine[13]. Born on 13 Apr 1733 in Colchester, New London CT.
On 14 Jul 1756 when Catherine was 23, she married **Daniel ISHAM Sr.**[13] in Colchester, New London CT.

xi. Noah[13]. Born in 1738 in Colchester, New London CT. Noah died 28 Feb 1809; at 71.
On 18 Apr 1768 when Noah was 30, he first married **Esther KELLOG**[13], daughter of Silas KELLOG, in Colchester, New London CT. Born 22 Oct 1741. Esther died on 18 Dec 1771; she was 30. In 1774 when Noah was 36, he second married **Tabitha SHAYLOR**[13], daughter of Ebenezer SHAYLOR. Born ca 1753. Tabitha died 1 Aug 1815; she was 62.

27

5. Jonathan FOOTE[13] was born on 23 Mar 1715 in Colchester, New London CT. Jonathan died in Lee MA, on 11 Nov 1803; he was 88. He was buried in Lee MA.

On 25 May 1749 when Jonathan was 34, he first married **Sarah FENNER**[13], daughter of John FENNER, in Colchester, New London CT. Born ca 1730 in Saybrook CT, Sarah died in Lee MA, on 27 Sep 1791[19], she was 61. She was buried in Lee MA.

They had the following children:

              i.   Martha Freelove[13]. Born on 11 Mar 1750. 25 May1770 when she was 19, she married **Simeon WRIGHT**[13]. Born in Rutland VT.

              ii.   Jonathan Jr.[13] Born on 30 Mar 1752 in Colchester, New London CT. Jonathan died on 26 May 1837; he was 85[17]. On 23 Dec 1773 when Jonathan was 21, he married **Deliverance GIBBS**[13], daughter of Sylvanus GIBBS. Born ca 1751[17]. Deliverance died 20 Apr 1828[17]; she was 77[17].

              iii.   Fenner[13]. Born on 5 Oct 1754. Fenner died on 27 Apr 1847; he was 92[17]. On 11 Mar 1779 when Fenner was 24, he married **Sarah WILCOX**[13], daughter of Peter WILCOX. Born ca 1764[17]. Sarah died on 14 Jan 1840; she was 76[17].

              iv.   Sarah[13]. Born on 12 Jan 1758. Ca 1778 when Sarah was 19, she married **Jesse CLARK**[13] in Lee MA. Born in Lee MA.

              v.   David[13]. Born on 4 Sep 1760. On 12 Jan 1785 when David was 24, he married **Betsey HAMBLIN**[1], daughter of Job HAMBLIN, in Lee MA. Born ca 1764. Betsey died on 10 Jan 1844; she was 80.

6   vi.   Asahel Sr. (22 Apr 1763-8 Mar 1841)

              vii.   Lovisa[13]. Born in 1765. Lovisa died on 17 Mar 1840; she was 75.

              viii. Dr. Solomon[1]. Born ca 1768 Solomon died on 29 Oct 1811; he was 43. In 1798 when Solomon was 30, he married

Betsey **CROSSETT**[1], daughter of Archibald CROSSETT. Born ca 1771. Betsey died on 13 Aug 1845; she was 74.
On 21 Jun 1792 when Jonathan was 77, he second married the widow **Temperance (Holly) STANLEY** in nearby Tyringham[12]. Temperance died in 1812.

Sixth Generation

----

6. Asahel FOOTE Sr.[1] was born on 22 Apr 1763 in Colchester, New London CT. Asahel died in Lee MA, on 8 Mar 1841 at 77. He was buried in Lee MA.
On 21 Aug 1793 when Asahel was 30, he married **Anna ABBOTT**[1], daughter of Seth ABBOTT & Martha. Born ca 1771 in probably Cornwall VT, Anna died in Lee MA, on 21 Jan 1820; she was 49. She was buried in Lee MA.

They had the following children:

i. Sarah Ann[1]. Born on 2 Apr 1794.
On 17 Sep 1817 when Sarah Ann was 23, she married **Henry CHAPMAN**[19]. Born in Becket MA.

ii. Elizabeth[1]. Born on 25 Dec 1795. Elizabeth died on 12 Jan 1831; she was 35[17].
On 7 Oct 1823 when Elizabeth was 27, she married **Lucius CROCKER**[1]. Born in Lee MA.

iii. Lyman[1]. Born on 9 Jul 1798. Lyman died on 5 May 1862; he was 63[18].
Resided in Lee MA, inherited the house of Jonathan and Asahel, Sr.
In Oct 1823 when Lyman was 25, he married **Emily FAIRCHILD**[1], daughter of Daniel FAIRCHILD. Born on 8 Sep 1800[18]. Emily died on 3 May 1863; she was 62[18].

iv. Charles[1]. Born on 12 May 1800. Charles died in Cleveland OH, on 9 Aug 1888; he was 88. Buried Woodlawn Cemetery, Cleveland OH. In 1831 when Charles was 30, he married **Marcia HUNTER**[1], daughter of Samuel

HUNTER. Marcia died on 12 Jun 1885.

v.   Amanda[1]. Born on 13 Jan 1803.
In Sep 1844 when Amanda was 41, she married **Spelman PELTON**[1]. Born on 8 Oct 1789. Spelman died in Clarksfield OH, on 10 Feb 1875; he was 85.

7   vi.   Deacon Asahel Jr. (16 Dec 1804-15 Jul 1882)

vii.   Anna[1]. Born on 16 Dec 1804. Asahel's twin sister.
On 4 Mar 1825 when Anna was 20, she married **Daniel G. WHITON Esq.**[19] son of Gen. Joseph WHITON (ca 1759-1828) & Amanda GARFIELD (ca 1775-1847) [12,], in Lee MA. Born on 20 Mar 1801 in Lee MA.

viii.   Lydia[1]. Born on 13 Sep 1807.
On 29 Dec 1829 when Lydia was 22, she married **Isaac BASSETT**. Born ca 1797 in Lee MA[25].

Seventh Generation
----

7. Deacon Asahel FOOTE Jr.[1] was born on 16 Dec 1804 in Lee MA. Asahel died in Williamstown MA, on 15 Jul 1882; he was 77[1]. He was buried in 1882 in East Lawn Cemetery, Williamstown MA.
On 14 Aug 1828 when Asahel was 23, he married **Mary SMEDLEY**[2] in Williamstown MA. Born on 29 Oct 1804 in Williamstown MA[26], Mary died in Williamstown MA, on 15 Aug 1876[26]; she was 71.

They had the following children:

i.   Harriet ("Hattie") Hillsgrove. Born on 8 Sep 1830 in St. Albans VT[1]. Harriet ("Hattie") Hillsgrove died in Springfield OH, on 27 Apr 1876; she was 45[1].
On 17 Nov 1853 when Harriet ("Hattie") Hillsgrove was 23, she married **Dr. Henry Hill SEYS**[1], son of John SEYS & Ann OSBORN[1]. Born on 13 Oct 1830 in Ogdensburg NY, Henry Hill died in Springfield OH, on 17 Jun 1904; he was 73. He was a surgeon during the Civil War[1],

then practiced medicine for 51 years in Springfield OH, 1853-1904.

They had two children, both born in Springfield OH: a daughter, Mary ("Minnie") Ellen[1], born 4 Aug 1854, who married **Edwin Dumont BUSS** on 23 Nov 1875[9] and had two daughters, Harriet Foote, born 30 Nov 1876[1] and Mabel Buell, born 22 Jul 1880[1], who married **Thomas Conrad DODGE** on 5 Jun 1917 in Bakersfield CA[1]. Neither daughter had children. John Henry, the son of Harriet and Henry, was born on 30 May 1857[1] and died in Murfreesboro TN on 5 Jun 1864, at age 7 of consumption, following measles. He had lived with his mother in the Foote homestead in Williamstown MA during the Civil War, and his death was bitterly mourned by his Williamstown family[2].

ii.   Mary Haines[1]. Born on 8 May 1834 in Williamstown MA. Mary Haines died on 7 Mar 1927; she was 92[5]. Buried in Mountain View Cemetery, Altadena. Never married.

iii. Ellen Maria[1]. Born on 3 Jul 1836 in Williamstown MA. Ellen Maria died on 12 Jun 1930; she was 93[5]. Buried in Mountain View Cemetery, Altadena CA- no marker. Res. Sierra Madre CA. On 17 Nov 1859 when Ellen Maria was 23, she married **Rev. James ORTON**[1]. Born in 1830 in LeRoy NY. James died in Lake Titicaca, Peru, on 25 Sep 1877; he was 47. Rev. Orton was a Presbyterian minister. From 1869-1877 he was on the faculty of Vassar College, as Chair of Natural History. He made 3 trips of exploration in the Andes Mountains in South America for the Smithsonian Institution, which houses many of his finds. Vassar Alumnae erected a memorial monument at his place of burial[1,6].

They had four children: Anna Bell, born 23 Jun 1862[1] in Thomaston ME, died 21 Feb 1952 in Pasadena CA, buried in Mountain View Cemetery, Altadena CA[5]; Susan Robinson, born 27 Jan 1865[1] in Brighton NY, died 6 May 1945, graduated from Vassar and taught music at the Orton School for Girls, buried in Mountain View Cemetery, Altadena CA[5]; Mary Blossom, born 4 Nov 1866[1] in Brighton NY, died 20 Jul 1885[1], buried in Williamstown MA[1]; Albert Lossing, born 4 Aug 1872 in Poughkeepsie NY[1], died 7 May 1908, buried in Mountain View Cemetery, Altadena CA[5].

None of the four children married, but Anna Bell, who attended Vassar, adopted a child when she was at least 45, while head of the classical prep school for girls she founded in 1890 in Pasadena. She also was a charter member of the Pasadena YWCA, and attended the unveiling of her father's monument at Lake Titicaca[6]. Her adopted daughter, **Katharine Mary** was born on 4 Jun 1907, died 6 Feb 1973, and was buried in Mountain View Cemetery, Altadena CA[5]. Katharine Mary first married **Alexander Houston MACDOUGAL**, died 28 Mar 1932 and was buried in Mountain View Cemetery, Altadena CA[5]. They had a son, **Alexander Stewart ORTON-MACDOUGAL**[6], who had two children, **Lauren** and **Brinn (Brian?)**[6]. Nothing is known of this branch. Katharine Mary married second **John Alexander SHANKS**, born 15 Aug 1913, died 4 Feb 1974, buried in Mountain View Cemetery, Altadena CA[5].

iv.   *Charles Rollin*[3]. Born on 2 Jun 1838 in Williamstown MA. Charles Rollin died in Pasadena CA, on 14 Mar 1924; he was 85. Buried in Mt. View Cemetery, Altadena CA. On 17 Oct 1872 when Charles Rollin was 34,

he married **Sarah Caroline COLE**[3], daughter of
Harvey Towner COLE (1810-1892) & Caroline
Augusta WATERMAN (1817-1881), in
Williamstown MA. Born on 18 Apr 1842 in
Whitehall NY. Sarah Caroline died in Pasadena
CA, on 18 Jan 1929; she was 86. Buried in
Mountain View Cemetery, Altadena CA.

v.   Catherine ("Kitty") Lewis[1]. Born on 26 Sep
1841 in Williamstown MA[1]. Catherine
("Kitty") Lewis died on 16 Jul 1922; she was
80[5]. Buried in Mountain View Cemetery,
Altadena CA. Never married.

***For further information about the descendants of Deacon Asahel
and Mary (Smedley) Foote's son, Charles Rollin, see George Clapp's
<u>The Ancestors and Descendants of Harvey Towner and Caroline
(Waterman) Cole</u>, pp 223-234 & pp 249-251.**

SEE SOURCE LIST AT END OF BOOK

Foote: Nathaniel, the "gateway ancestor," to Charles Rollin

Nathaniel I
b 1592 Colchester, England - d 1644 Wethersfield CT
1633 emigrated to Watertown MA
1636 to Wethersfield CT

Nathaniel II
b 1620 Colchester, England
1633 to Watertown MA
1636 to Wethersfield CT
d 1655 Hadley MA (age 35)

Nathaniel III
b 1647 Wethersfield CT
1672 to Hatfield MA
1674 to Springfield MA
ca 1675 to Stratford CT
1676 to Branford CT
1677 to Wethersfield CT
d 1702 Wethersfield CT

Josiah
b 1688 Wethersfield CT
d 1778 Colchester CT

Jonathan
b 1715 Colchester CT
briefly to Saybrook CT
ca. 1770 Lee MA
d 1803 Lee MA

Asahel, Sr
b 1763 Colchester CT
d 1841 Lee MA

Asahel, Jr
b 1804 Lee MA
1879 briefly to Pasadena CA
d 1882 Williamstown MA

Charles Rollin Foote
b 1838 Williamstown MA
1873 to Rosamond IL
1879 to Pasadena CA
d 1924 Pasadena CA

Foote ancestry from the immigrant ancestor, Nathaniel, to Charles Rollin Foote, compiled from Abram W. Foote's Foote Family[1].

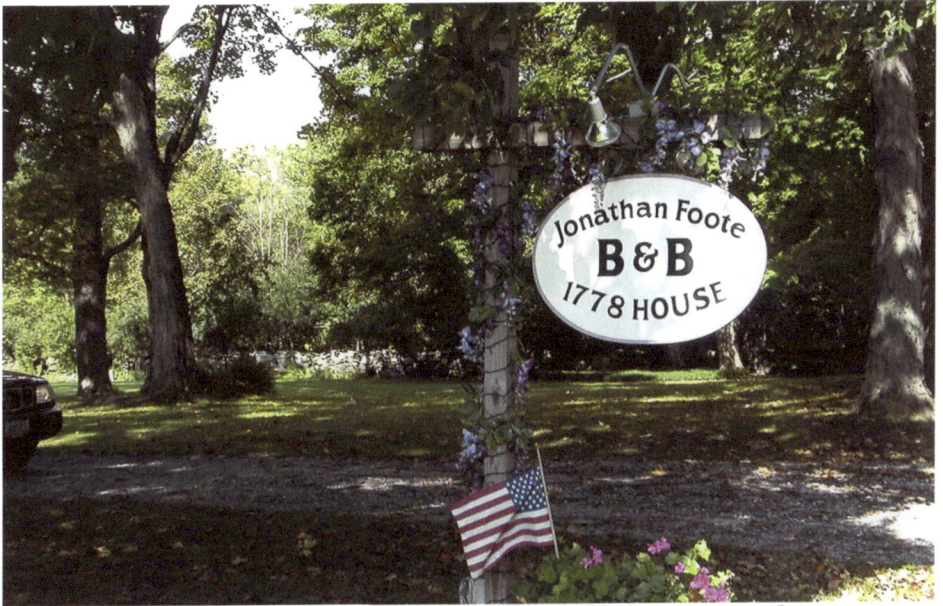

Driveway to Jonathan Foote's homestead, built in 1778 in Lee MA[15], now a B&B. Photo 2003[35].

Rear of the 1778 Jonathan Foote House, original house plus later porch on the left, with several additions to the ell on the right. Photo 2003[35].

At some point prior to 1884[21-679] a small tavern wing was added to the left of the main 1778 Jonathan Foote House. Photo 2003[35].

Hearth in the tavern of the 1778 Jonathan Foote House. Photo 2003[35].

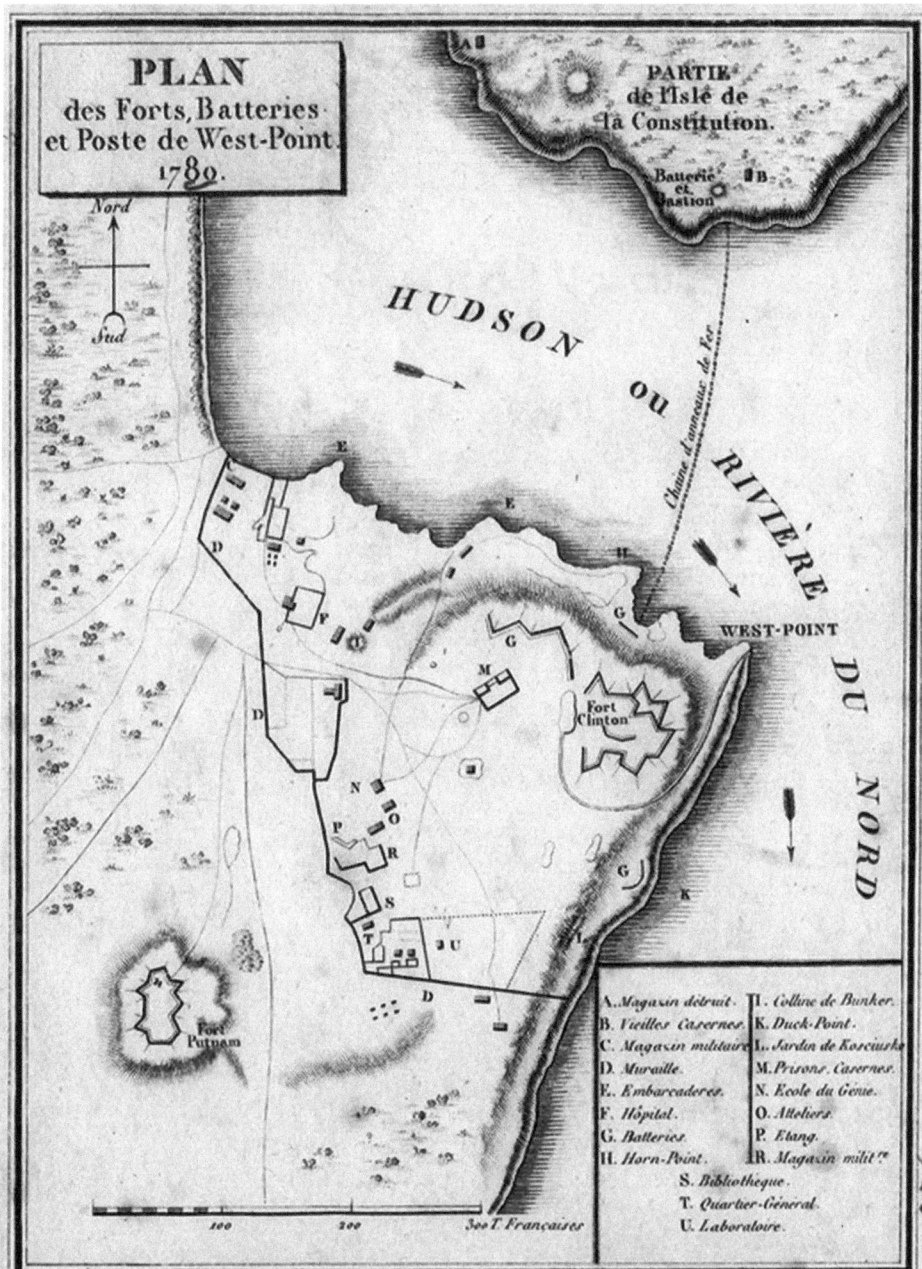

PLAN
des Forts, Batteries
et Poste de West-Point.
1780.

Nord

Sud

PARTIE
de l'Isle de
la Constitution.

Batterie
et
Bastion

B

HUDSON ou RIVIÈRE DU NORD

Chaine d'anneaux de Fer

WEST-POINT

Fort
Clinton

Fort
Putnam

A. Magasin détruit.	I. Colline de Bunker.
B. Vieilles Casernes.	K. Duck-Point.
C. Magasin militaire	L. Jardin de Kosciusko
D. Muraille.	M. Prisons, Casernes.
E. Embarcaderes.	N. École du Génie.
F. Hôpital.	O. Ateliers.
G. Batteries.	P. Étang.
H. Horn-Point.	R. Magasin milit.re
S. Bibliothèque.	
T. Quartier-Général.	
U. Laboratoire.	

100   200   300 T. Françaises

Local legend in Lee MA maintains that Asahel Foote, Sr. was present at the laying of the chain across the Hudson River at West Point to block British forces[28-136], as seen in this "Map of West Point Defenses[41]" which includes the Great Chain, Constitution Island, Fort Clinton, and Fort Putnam.

37

Asahel Foot, Sr.'s grave in Lee MA, with Revolutionary
War commemorative marker[17-29].

Asahel Foote, Jr., possibly taken at the wedding of his son, Charles Rollin,
17 Oct 1872[35].

Portrait of Solomon Foot, which hangs over the mantel in the 1778 Jonathan Foote House. Solomon (1802-1866) was Asahel, Jr.'s first cousin. Between 1851–1866, he was a US Senator from VT, and President Pro Tempore of the Senate during the Civil War[1-113].

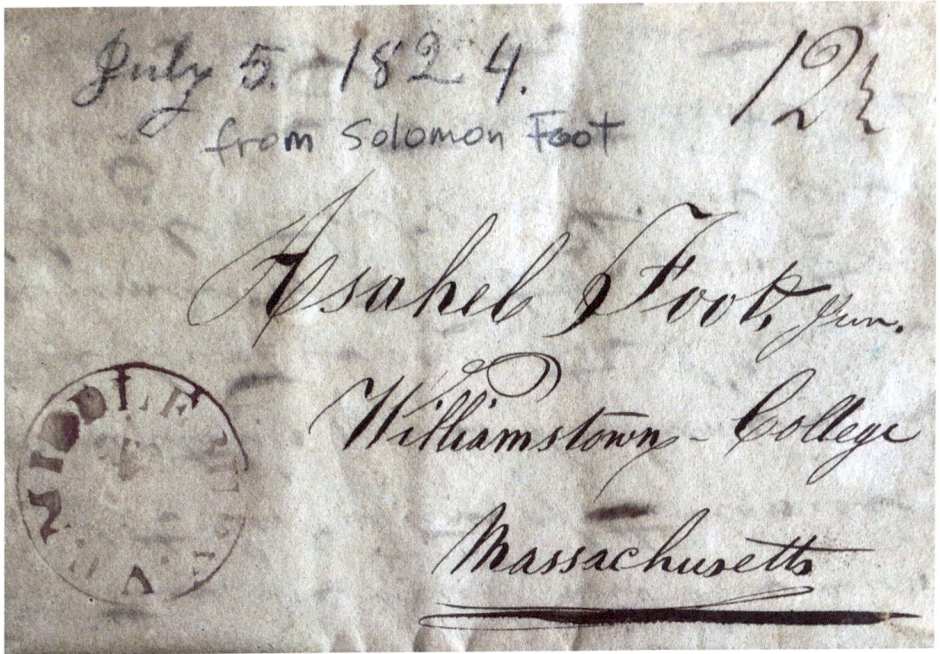

Early letters[31] from Solomon Foot at Middlebury College to Asahel, Jr. at Williamstown College address him as "Foot." Soon, however, Asahel had dandified his last name by adding a final "e."

Commencement at Williams College took place on Wednesday, the 5th inst. The day was fine, which gave an opportunity for a much larger and more brilliant audience to attend, than we have ever before witnessed on similar occasions, at this College. — The following was the order of exercises : —

MORNING.

1. Sacred Music.
2. Prayer by the President.
3. Salutatory Oration in Latin. — JAMES BALLARD, Charlemont.
4. *Oration.* — The importance of high aims. — GEORGE HUBBELL TRACY, Troy, N. Y.
5. *Dissertation.* — The Inquisition. — SAMUEL WILCOX, Hartford, Con.
6. *Conference.* — Henry Martyn and Gordon Hall. — WILLIAM BRADLEY, Lee, DAVID DOWNS GREGORY, Sand Lake, N. Y.

MUSIC.

7. *Dissertation.* — The claims of the Aborigines. — BARNABAS PHINNEY, Lee.
8. *Oration.* — Influence of climate on physical and mental constitution. — BENJAMIN FRANKLIN HOXSEY, Williamstown.
9. *Oration.* — Triumphs of Truth. — JOSEPH MERRILL SADD, New Hartford, Con.
10. *Disputation.* — The expediency of attempting an entire suppression of the use of ardent spirits. — ORSAMUS TINKER, Worthington ; ASAHEL FOOTE, Lee.

MUSIC.

11. *Oration.* — Oriental Poetry. — OSCAR HARRIS, Goshen, N. Y.
12. *Conference.* — Reputation as depending on Genius, Application, and Circumstances. — GEORGE WHITEFIELD HATHAWAY, Freetown ; WILLIAM LEWIS, New Windsor, N. Y. ; BARUCH BUTLER BECKWITH, Great Barrington.
13. *Philosophical Oration.* — Light. — JOSEPH ANDERSON, Shelburne.

EVENING.

14. Sacred Music.

Detail listing Asahel as a participant in a Disputation about prohibition, from the program of the 1827 Williams College Commencement[33-479].

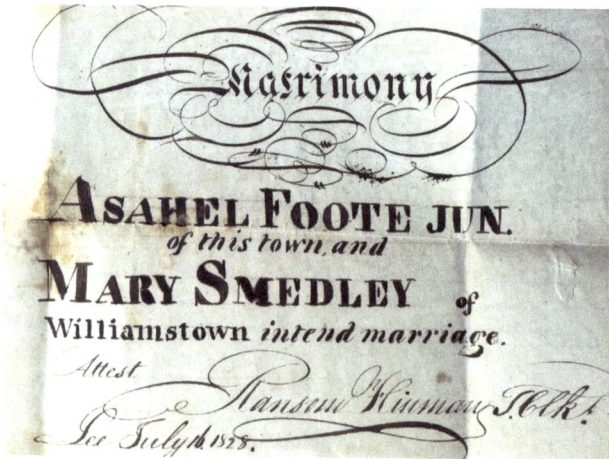

Intentions of Marriage[19-191] of Asahel Foote and Mary Smedley, published 16 July 1828, Lee MA[35].

Mary Smedley Foote, possibly taken at the wedding of her son, Charles Rollin, 17 Oct 1872[35].

CATALOGUE, &c.

OF THE

Franklin County Grammar School,

St. Albans, Vermont,

For the Quarter ending August 17th, 1830.

Ladies' Department.

Superintendant.....Miss NANCY SWIFT.

STUDENTS.

Daphne P. Ball,	Bakersfield.	Harriet B. Hall,	St. Albans.	Fidelia A. Lock,	St. Albans.	Harriet M. Smith,	St. Albans.
Hepsibah R. Barber,	Swanton.	Sarah F. Holmes,	Fairfax.	Sally Lord,	Cambridge.	Lucinda W. Spaulding,	Swanton.
Ann Eliza Brainerd,	St. Albans.	Emily S. Houghton,	St. Albans.	Frances E. Morgan,	Essex.	Amanda E. Squires,	St. Albans.
Emily A. Brown,	do.	Harriet N. Hoyt,	do.	Cynthia J Peirce,	St. Johns, L. C.	Catharine Swift,	do.
Maria Chandler,	do.	Lucy Huntington,	Vergennes.	Augusta E. Randall,	St. Albans.	Sarah Wheat,	do.
Melissa M. Dexter,	do.	Frances E. Janes,	St. Albans.	Ann S. Read,	Cambridge.	Sarah M. Warner,	Cambridge.
Mary Dutcher,	do.	Mary E. Judson,	Sheldon.	Lodoiska A. Robinson,	St. Albans.	Caroline M. Whiting,	St. Albans.
Mary C. Field,	Peterborough. N. H.	Julia A. Keeler,	Grand Isle.	Olive A. Robinson,	do.	Elizabeth S. Wilkins,	do.
Sarinda Fowler,	St. Albans.	Harriet Kingman,	St. Albans.	Elizabeth Seymour,	do.		

Gentlemen's Department.

Superintendant.....ASAHEL FOOTE, A. B.

Assistant.....Aaron M. Colton.

STUDENTS.

John Anderson,	St. Albans.	William R. Ferriss,	St. Albans.	Chester Keyes,	Sheldon.	Wright Sherman,	Fairfield.
Alvin Barnard,	Malone, N. Y.	Lyman Fisk,	Fairfax.	Franklin King,	Burlington.	Horatio Smith,	St. Albans.
John Barnard,	Claremont, N. H.	Dan Foster,	St. Albans.	William Lawrence,	St. Albans.	Worthington Smith,	do.
Edgar M. Burton,	St. Albans.	Hampton Foster,	Sheldon.	David L. Lewis,	Noyan, L. C.	John G. Smith,	do.
Solomon Bingham, jr.	Noyan, L. C	Hannibal H. Gould,	Fairfield.	Charles Marvin,	Franklin.	George N. Smith,	Swanton.
Stephen H. Campbell,	St. Albans.	Charles H. Hall,	St. Albans.	Francis Marvin,	do.	Lewis Sowles,	Alburgh.
Seymour S. Carr,	Franklin.		Sheldon.	Jonathan Marvin,	do.	John A. Spooner,	Windsor.
Caleb Clapp,	Montgomery.	Edwin M. Hennessy,	St. Albans.	Josiah B. Maynard,	do.	George S. Swift,	St. Albans.
Alvin Church,	St. Albans.	Frederick Houghton,	do.	Henry B. Moulthrop,	Burlington.	William Swift,	do.
Lewis Dean,	do.	Thomas S. Hubbard,	Franklin.	Theodore Randall,	St. Albans.	Ebenezer M. Toof,	St. Armand, L. C.
Rodney Dodge,	do.	James L. Hunt,	St. Albans.	Sterling P. Searle,	Berkshire.	Milton M. Torrey,	Georgia.
Horace Easton,	do.	Henry B. Janes,	do.	Henry E. Seymour,	St. Albans.	John Watson, jr.,	St. Albans.
John Farrar, jun.	do.	Franklin Keeler,	do.	Horatio Seymour,	do.	Jacob Wead,	Sheldon.
						Gibson T. Williams,	Enosburgh.

* This name is omitted for *flagrant misconduct.*

SUMMARY—Ladies, 35,—Gentlemen in the Languages, 18,—do. English Branches, 35,—Total, 88.

The Superintendants of this Institution deem it proper, as they now design remaining permanently in their present sphere of labour, to acquaint the public, briefly, with the views they entertain, and with the plan of operations they intend pursuing. Education we consider as involving its distinct constituent *parts*; the principal of which are, first, *instruction*, second, *discipline*; the single object of them both united, being the formation of well founded principles of action. To impart instruction with success, two things are requisite; the voluntary and absorbed attention of the pupil, and precise conceptions of the nature of the truth at any time investigated. To insure the first of these, the frequent employment of a suitable variety of well selected motives will be commonly sufficient; and the second may be equally effected by requiring of the scholar correctly to communicate, in a familiar language, (not however without aid, if needed,) every thing admitting proof within his range of studies. Discipline we cannot "put asunder" from instruction; for the value of them both, requires their being "joined together." It is this which must secure the youth from indolent, irregular, and vicious dispositions, and the unrestrained indulgence of improper appetites and hurtful passions; check the overforwardness of the assuming and pedantic, give encouragement to the desponding, and inspire the timorous with confidence. Whatever natural defect may be discovered, there must be an essay to remove it, and produce its opposite. To make ourselves acquainted with the human mind and heart, and to discover the most simple and efficient methods of developing the noblest powers and qualities of each, will be our unremitted effort. Such, we imagine, will be found the only proper scheme of education. Not to polish the exterior, to mar the graces nature has herself perfected, but to cultivate the head and heart, will be our object: to induce the habit of correct and independent thinking, (for from thought originate all actions, good and bad,) to predispose our pupils for a life of persevering application, and to qualify them for extensive usefulness.

St. Albans, August 12, 1830.

QUARTERS, VACATIONS, TUITION, AND BOARD.

The ensuing year will be divided into four quarters—the first commencing on the second Wednesday of September, and continuing twelve weeks,—the second on the second Wednesday of December, do.—the third on the second Wednesday of March, continuing eleven weeks—the fourth on the second Wednesday of June, do.

Tuition for the common English studies, 25 cents per week—for the higher branches in English, and for Ancient Languages, 33 do.—and for Modern Languages, 37½ do.

Good Board may be obtained, within convenient distances from the Academy, for $1 25 to $1 50 per week.

BOOKS USED.

Scholars who may purchase books previous to entering the School, are desired to furnish themselves with the following authors. Mental Arithmetic, Colburn's, Practical do., Adams'; Modern Geography, Woodbridge's, Ancient do., Willard's; English Grammer, Greenleaf's, Latin do., Gould's, Greek do., Goodrich's; Rhetoric, Blair's; Logic, Hedge's; History, Whelpley's Compend; Natural Philosophy, Blake's, Moral do., Parkhurst's; Chymistry, Comstock's; Surveying, Flint's; Algebra, Colburn's.

FALL AND SPRING QUARTERS.

During these two quarters, it will be our object to bestow particular attention on Young Gentlemen and Ladies who design instructing Common Schools, and thus to lend our efforts in advancing those material promoters of our national prosperity.

ASSISTANTS.

Competent Assistants will at all times be employed when necessary, and our patrons may assure themselves, that no endeavors will be wanting to repay their favours, by the just attention given to their children.

Flyer for the Franklin County Grammar School in St. Albans, VT where Asahel was Superintendent of the Gentlemen's Department, dated 12 Aug 1830[35].

MR. FOOTE'S
SEMINARY FOR BOYS,
AT
WILLIAMSTOWN, MASS.

This School (which has been in successful operation for the last five years,) possesses the following characteristics :—

1. In its organization it aims to combine, with the most approved systems of physical and mental development, the social and moral advantages of a well-regulated Christian Family.

2. In consistency with this organization, the number of Pupils, including the children of the Principal, is expected never to exceed *fifteen ;* and in the admission of these a constant regard is had to moral qualification.

3. It is designed to sustain a decidedly Religious character. Besides making the Bible their text-book on the Sabbath, the Pupils daily repeat from memory a given portion of Scripture ; and from the same source are constantly presented motives to the pursuit of "whatsoever is true, just, lovely, and of good report."

4. Its location is one of uncommon healthfulness, of great natural beauty, and peculiarly exempt from scenes of immorality. It is also connected with an excellent farm establishment, which promotes the welfare of the Pupils in various ways—presenting them with an opportunity of witnessing the operations of agriculture in all their variety, giving them full scope for free and invigorating exercise, and furnishing their table with a constant abundance of the most wholesome articles of vegetable food.

5. Its Patrons, if resident anywhere on the Hudson, are freed from the inconvenience and expense of accompanying their sons to and from School,—the Principal making it his uniform practice to take his Pupils from, and return them to the place of their residence, at the commencement and close of each term.

6. The course of instruction pursued is systematic, thorough, and practical—the constant aim of the Principal being to secure correctness and efficiency of character to his Pupils : and parents and guardians may be assured that no becoming effort will be spared to promote *every* prominent interest of those committed to his care—to render them contented and happy—to guard them from accident and disease—to secure them from temptation and vice—to lead them to the formation of *correct habits,* not only of thinking, but of feeling *and of action*—in short, to train them up to that healthful, vigorous, and *properly directed* exercise of *all* their faculties, in which consists the real greatness and the highest happiness of every rational being.

The division of the year is into two Terms, of 22 weeks each ; the one to commence on the second Thursday in May, the other on the second Thursday in November, each to be succeeded by a vacation of four weeks.

The annual expense of tuition and board, the latter to include lodging, washing, mending, fuel and light, is $175, payable semi-annually in advance. An exception to this rule is made in favour of gentlemen furnishing two sons at once, who are allowed a deduction of $25 on each.
ASAHEL FOOTE.

RECOMMENDATIONS.

Mr. Asahel Foote graduated at this College in 1827, and has spent all his time since in public Academies. I have entire confidence in Mr. Foote in all respects, and believe that he will give distinguished satisfaction to those who commit their sons to his care.
Williams College, March 16th, 1833.
E. D. GRIFFIN.

I have been intimately acquainted with Mr. Asahel Foote from his earliest years ; and am happy in being able to give assurance that he has ever sustained an unblemished reputation, and for several years a consistent Christian character. Since he graduated, he has been employed in instructing youth in the various branches of science, and has acquired an uncommon celebrity as a teacher. I most cheerfully recommend him as one eminently qualified to take the charge of youth, and prepare them for admission into our Colleges.
Lee, February 28th, 1833.
ALVAN HYDE, Minister of the Gospel in Lee.

The undersigned have been intimately acquainted with Mr. Asahel Foote for a course of years. During this time he has sustained the character of a consistent Christian, and of a faithful and successful teacher of youth. He is a sound, practical scholar, has been long in the business of teaching, and has fitted numbers of Students for admission into most of the Colleges in this section of the country. His present establishment is somewhat peculiar in its organization, and affords distinguished advantages :—its location also is beautiful and healthy, and is remarkably free from the corrupting influence of immoral example.

In assiduous attention to his charge, and in carrying out the details of a well-matured system of physical, mental, and moral training for Boys, we think Mr. Foote can have few equals, and perhaps no superiors in the country.
Williams College, April 10th, 1838.

Mark Hopkins,	Joseph Alden,
Ebenezer Kellogg,	Edward Lasell,
Albert Hopkins,	Ebenezer Emmons.

P. S.—Two regular lines of stages form a daily communication between Williamstown and Troy, (36 miles,) and render the former easily accessible to all places on the Hudson. Communications addressed by mail to the Principal, at Williamstown, will at all times receive immediate attention and prompt returns.
ASAHEL FOOTE.

Flyer for Mr. Foote's Seminary for Boys, established by Asahel in Mary's parents' Williamstown home, dated 1838[35].

Memorandum of Special Fruits,

Pears.

The Back Row, West side of Deciduous Orchard, is taken for Row No 1, & from that the Rows are numbered East, and the trees counted North.

Homestead – 5th Row, 5th tree, & 11th Row, & 11th Row, 14th tree.

Sheldon – 6th Row, 6th (& 7th?) tree,

Doyenné d'Eté, in the 8th Row, 10th tree (W. branch) & in the 12th tree, same row, & the 14th tree of the 7th Row.

Flemish Beauty in the last named tree.

Beurré Giffard (according to Watts) in the 10th Row, 16th tree.

Beurré d'Anjou – 16th Row, 13th tree

Leckel, & L's Leckel, 14th Row, 14th tree,

Detail of a schematic plan of extensive fruit orchards, hand written by Asahel on the back of a letter from a pupil's father, dated 11 Sep 1834. Even though his school was just getting off the ground, he may already have been dreaming of his later horticultural pursuits[35].

FOOTE'S PRIZE ESSAY.

ESSAY

ON THE

MANUFACTURE OF MANURES,

AND THE

APPLICATION OF THE SAME TO THE DIFFERENT VARIETIES OF SOILS.

BY ASAHEL FOOTE.

READ BEFORE THE BERKSHIRE AGRICULTURAL SOCIETY.

BOSTON:
PRINTED BY SAMUEL N. DICKINSON.
1843.

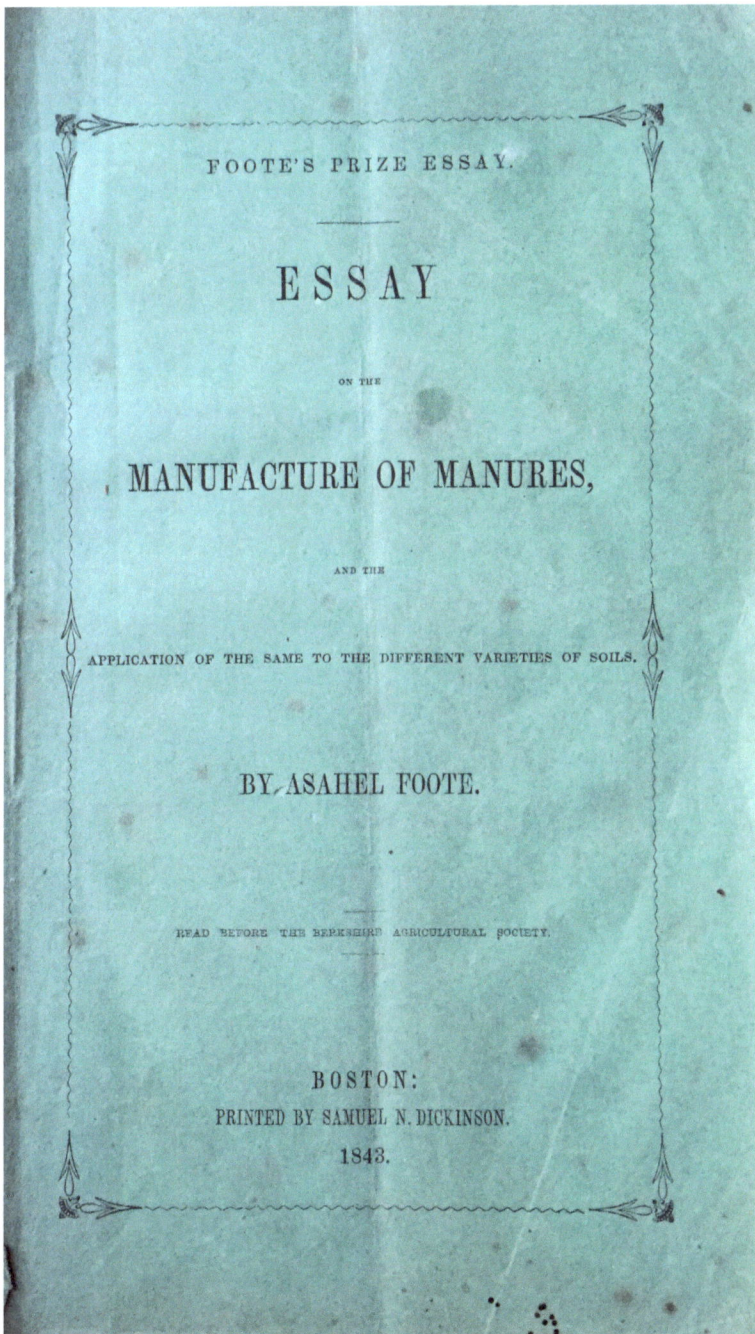

Foote's Prize Essay on the Manufacture of Manures, Boston: Printed by Samuel A. Dickinson, 1843. This essay won him two prizes from horticultural societies, one for $50[35].

AT THE
GREYLOCK NURSERIES,
IN WILLIAMSTOWN, MASS.,
—ARE PROPAGATED THE FOLLOWING VARIETIES OF—
FRUIT TREES,
MOST OF WHICH ARE READY FOR SALE THE PRESENT SEASON.

Cherries.

LIGHT COLORED.

1 American Amber,
2 Belle de Choisy,
3 Bigarreau,
4 Bowyer's Early Heart,
5 Burr's Seedling,
6 Butner's Yellow,
7 Coe's Transparent,
8 Downton,
9 Early White Heart,
10 Elton,
11 Flesh Colored Bigarreau,
12 Florence,
13 Harrison's Heart,
14 Hildesheim Bigarreau,
15 Holland Bigarreau,
16 Honey Heart,
17 Napoleon Bigarreau,
18 Sparhawk's Honey,
19 Sweet Montmorency,
20 White Heart,
21 White Ox Heart.

Quinces.

Apple or Orange for fruit, Angers for stocks.

Native Grapes.

Catawba,
Clinton,
Isabella,
Mt. Holyoke,
Purple Connecticut,
Virginia Creeper,
White Connecticut,

Gooseberries.

A variety of the best sorts, and of the different colors.

Currants.

A full assortment, including the Black English, and Black Naples, (fine for preserving, and exceedingly productive,)

PRICES AT RETAIL.—Apples, 20 cts.; Pears and Plums, 50 cts.; Cherries, 40 cts.; Quinces and Grapes, 25 cts.; Gooseberries and Currants, 12 1-2 cts. Apples by the hundred, $18.

The above prices will be varied in the case of extra large trees, new and rare sorts, and extra large orders.

Trees going to a distance will be packed in the securest manner, and delivered free of charge at the North Adams Depot. Charges for packing only to cover the cost of the materials.

NOTE.—The "American Pomological Congress" has adopted the terms "Good," "Very Good," "Best," to indicate the different grades of fruits that are really valuable. The proprietor is now making proof in his Experimental Orchards, of all the foregoing varieties; and hereafter all varieties falling in proof, below the standard of "Very Good," will be rejected from his Nursery Lists, and those alone retained which have given proof of superior excellence. ADDRESS

ASAHEL FOOTE, Proprietor.

Williamstown, March, 1852.

1852 Flyer for Greylock Nurseries (Asahel Foote, Proprietor) mail order and retail fruit tree stock[35].

48

Detail of an 1852 newspaper ad offering free catalogues from Asahel's Greylock Nurseries[35].

THE

FRUITS AND FRUIT-TREES

OF

AMERICA;

OR,

THE CULTURE, PROPAGATION, AND MANAGEMENT, IN THE
GARDEN AND ORCHARD, OF FRUIT-TREES GENERALLY;

WITH

DESCRIPTIONS OF ALL THE FINEST VARIETIES OF FRUIT, NATIVE
AND FOREIGN, CULTIVATED IN THIS COUNTRY.

By A. J. DOWNING,

CORRESPONDING MEMBER OF THE ROYAL BOTANIC SOCIETY OF LONDON; AND OF THE HORTICUL-
TURAL SOCIETIES OF BERLIN, THE LOW COUNTRIES, MASSACHUSETTS,
PENNSYLVANIA, INDIANA, CINCINNATI, ETC.

" What wondrous life is this I lead ?
Ripe apples drop about my head;
The luscious clusters of the vine
Upon my mouth do crush their wine ;
The nectarine and curious peach
Into my hands themselves do reach."
MARVELL.

SECOND REVISION AND CORRECTION, WITH LARGE ADDITIONS, BY

CHARLES DOWNING.

NEW YORK:
JOHN WILEY & SON, 2 CLINTON HALL, ASTOR PLACE.
1869.

The Fruits and Fruit-Trees of America…, A. J. Downing, New
York, John Wiley & Son, New York, 1869. This "bible" of the
horticultural world was personally inscribed to Asahel by the author[35].

Fruit nearly of medium size, roundish, a little depressed. Skin pale yellow. Stalk stout, an inch and a half long, planted in a rather deep cavity. Calyx set in a pretty deep basin. Flesh white, juicy, melting, sweet, and of very agreeable flavor. Only good. First of November.

FOOTE'S SECKEL.

Raised by Asahel Foote, of Williamstown, Mass., from seed of the Seckel. A very promising new variety, ripening a week or two later than its parent, and a little more vinous. Tree healthy, vigorous, more spreading than Seckel. Young wood dark rich brown.

Fruit small, oblate obtuse pyriform, yellow, shaded with brownish crimson in the sun, nearly covered with rich crimson russet. Stalk short, fleshy.

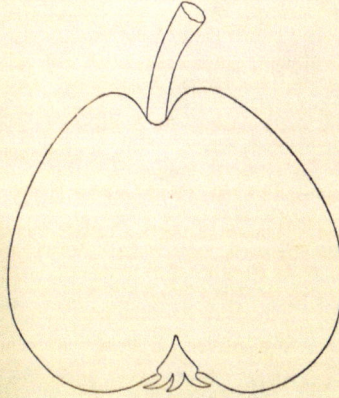

Foote's Seckel.

Cavity small. Calyx open. Basin medium, rather deep. Flesh whitish, fine, juicy, melting, sugary, slightly vinous. Very good. September

Foote's Seckel pear, propagated by Asahel, from The Fruits and Fruit-Trees of America..., p 765[35].

FOCHT.

A seedling of Lebanon Co., Pa. Tree forms a low open head, productive.

Fruit large, oblate, slightly conic, pale yellow, sometimes with a blush. Flesh white, tender, juicy, good, subacid. October, December. Excellent for culinary purposes.

FOOTE'S NONPAREIL.

Origin, farm of Jonathan Foote, Lee, Mass. Tree thrifty, vigorous, spreading, an annual bearer.

Fruit small, oblong conic truncated, yellow shaded and indistinctly splashed with crimson. Flesh firm, juicy, pleasant aromatic subacid. Very good. Core large. November.

Foote's Nonpareil apple, propagated by Asahel's grandfather, Jonathan, in Lee, from The Fruits and Fruit-Trees of America..., p 179[35].

51

Side entry and brick addition to the Orchards, presumably built in the mid-1830s, to provide more room for boarding students when Asahel's school was begun. Photo 1972[35].

Foote family group photo, ca 1856, labeled: Charles Rollin, Asahel, Katherine, Mary (Smedley), Mary. The thumbprint on the left presumably covered the third Foote daughter, Ellen. Harriet, the eldest, had already married and moved away[35].

At some point during Asahel's career as an orchardist, his extensive nursery property became known as The Orchards, instead of Greylock Nurseries. What is presumably one of his original apple trees was still standing in this 1972 photo[35].

This ca 1960 postcard affirms the name change to The Orchards, and shows the property's new use as a Motor Court, or motel[35].

The Orchards Motor Court even sported a swimming pool! Photo 1972[35].

By 1984 the Orchards was no longer painted white. The property had been sold as the site for a new hotel, also named The Orchards. The old house was moved around the corner, as captured by local photographer, Leith Colon[35].

The brick wing of The Orchards, re-located on its current site on Stratton Road. Photo 2003[35].

Front of the brick wing of The Orchards on Stratton Road. Photo 2003[35].

Original post and beam structure built between 1810-1820, to the rear of the brick wing. Photo 2003[35].

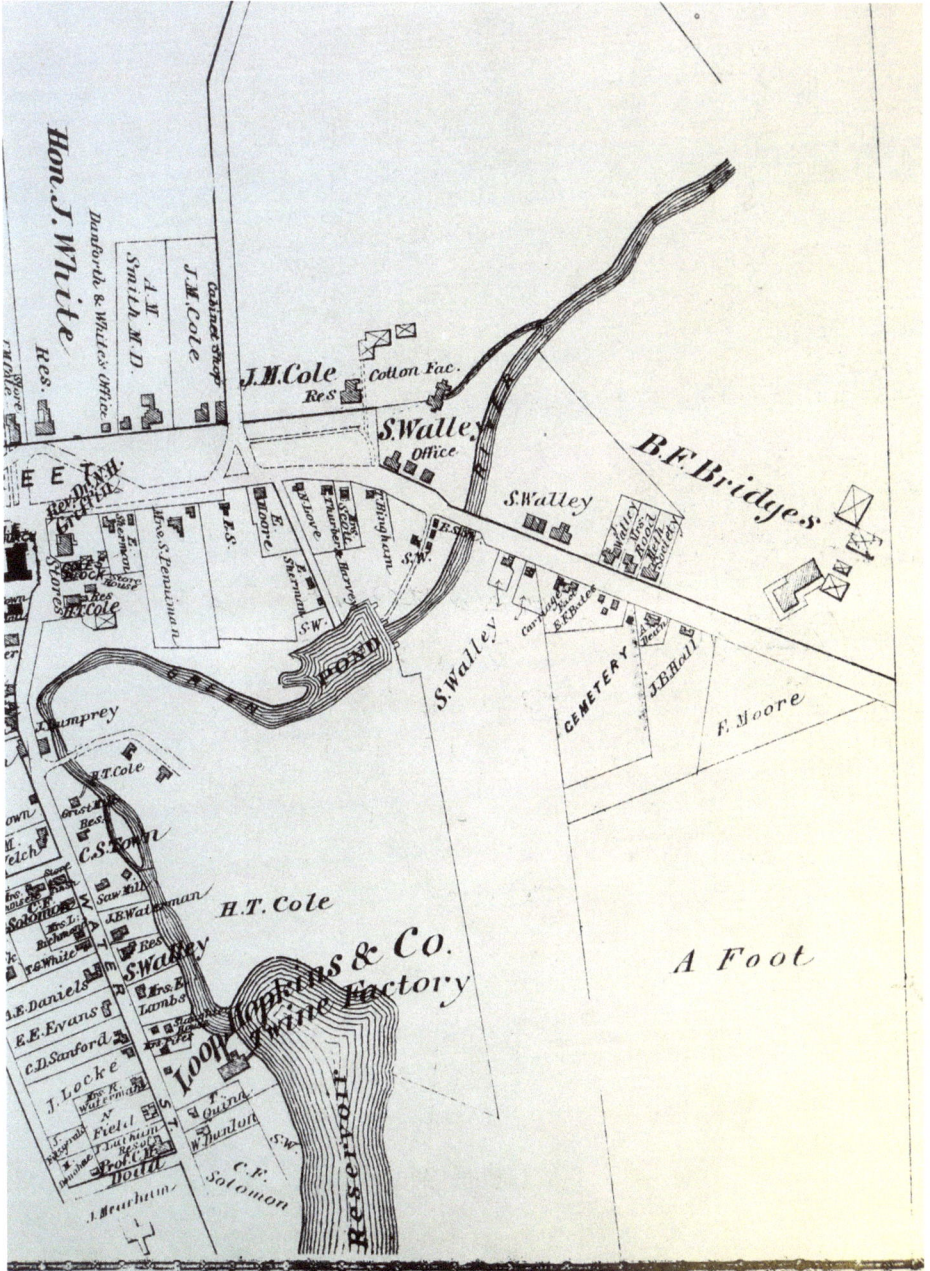

1876 map showing how the marriage of Charles Rollin Foote and Sarah Caroline Cole was truly the story of a young man marrying the girl next door. Detail of the neighboring properties of A. Foot and H. T. Cole, County Atlas of Berkshire Massachusetts[36].

Charles Rollin Foote, possibly taken at his wedding to Sarah Caroline Cole, 17 Oct 1872[35].

Charles Rollin Foote with his entire living family, all in Pasadena, ca 1900-1903. To Charles Rollin's right, widowed sister Ellen Orton, sister Kitty, daughter Ethelywn, Susan Orton (daughter of Ellen), sister Mary, Annie (Anna Belle) Orton (daughter of Ellen), wife Sarah Cole Foote[35].

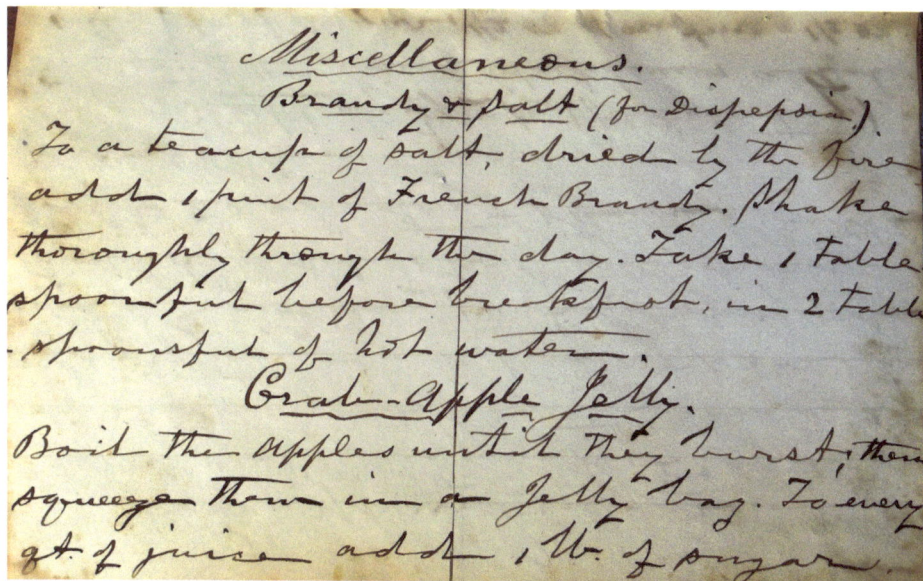

A treasure that was preserved by Charles Rollin and his descendants until the present day is a hand-bound, hand-written booklet of recipes (receipts as they were called in the mid-19th century) compiled by Asahel[35]. Taking brandy and salt prior to dinner to ward off indigestion might be worth a try!

Probably the original 1879 cottage of Charles Rollin Foote in Pasadena, moved to Orange Grove Ave ca1886, according to p 226 of <u>Ancestors and Descendants of Harvey Towner and Caroline (Waterman) Cole</u>..., by George W. Clapp[3].

One has to wonder how often and with what feelings the Pasadena Footes envisioned this idyllic view of their old home in Williamstown. 1889 by the Panoramic Map CD, MA, Vol II, US Historical Archive.

THE DEATH OF DEACON FOOTE.

The death of Asahel Foote occurred at his home in this village Saturday evening after many weeks illness since his return from Los Angelos county, Cal., the home of his son and for two years the home of the father. The death of Mr. Foote removes one of the old Williamstown residents and Williams college graduates, the record of whose life has from its earliest days been connected with Williamstown history and public spirit. Earnest interest in Williamstown, its business and social progress and the condition of its college was a prominent characteristic of the deceased and in his earlier years much of his labor was spent in public work and enterprise. He had been a member of both houses of the legislature, a county commissioner, a deacon of the Congregational church here for many years, and was always identified with town matters. After his purchase of the farm in Los Angelos, Cal., he moved there, but returned to Williamstown, on a visit, and the journey was too much for his strength. He was 78 years old, and leaves five children, four daughters and one son, the latter now in California. The funeral occurred Monday afternoon at his late residence, Rev. A. C. Sewall conducting the services.

Obituary of Asahel Foote, 20 Jul 1882, *The Adams Transcript*[39].

FOOTE SOURCES

1. Foote, Abram W. <u>Foote Family Comprising the Genealogy and History of Nathaniel Foote of Wethersfield, Conn. and his Descendants</u>. Vol. I originally printed Rutland VT: Marble City Press, 1907; Vol. II originally printed Burlington, Vermont, 1932. Both volumes reprinted by Laura Belle Foote Beekman and Clarance William Beekman, 5236 Geer Rd., Hughson, CA 95326, Gateway Press, Inc., Baltimore, 1981.
2. Family Records (with some inconsistencies) to be archived at NEHGS.
3. Clapp, George W. <u>Ancestors and Descendants of Harvey Towner and Caroline (Waterman) Cole of Williamstown MA 1810 - 1881</u>. Barrington RI: Presentation Press and Judith Bennett Wilson, 2002.
4. <u>A Southern California Paradise</u>. Edited and published by RWC Farnsworth, Pasadena, California, 1883.
5. Mountain View Cemetery, Altadena CA, Office Records.
6. California obituaries file, to be archived at NEHGS.
7. <u>Vital Records of Williamstown, Massachusetts, to the year 1850</u>. Boston, Mass.: Published by the New England Historic Genealogical Society at the Charge of the Eddy Town-Record Fund, 1907. Plus other local vital records, census data, etc.
8. "The Orchards," built ca 1810-1820, Smedley/Foote homestead until 1882. File of newspaper clippings, local histories and photographs, to be archived at NEHGS.
9. <u>The Berkshire Hills</u>. Compiled and Written by Members of the Federal Writers' Project of the Works Progress Administration for Massachusetts. New York and London: Funk and Wagnalls Company, 1939.
10. Henry H Seys letter, 25 Nov 1862, Schoff Civil War Collection, William L. Clement Library, University of Michigan.
11. Brooks, Robert R.R., Editor. <u>Williamstown The First Two Hundred Years 1753-1953 and Twenty Years Later 1953-1973</u>, Second Edition, Williamstown Historical Commission, 1974.
12. <u>Records of the Town of Lee from its incorporation to A.D. 1801</u>. All the extant records of the Town Clerks, Town Treasurers, Hopland School District and Congregational Church for that period; also Inscriptions from the Cemeteries; with an Appendix containing a brief account of the town's incorporation, State and County Taxes, and other matters relating to the early history of the town. Lee, Mass.: Press of the *Valley Gleaner*, 1900.

13. Curtis, Ellwood Count, compiler. <u>The Descendants of Nathaniel Foote (1592-1644) and Elizabeth Deming (1595-1683)</u>. Cedar Falls, Iowa: Galactic Press, 2012. (Curtis' work is a scrupulous compilation of both of Abram Foote's volumes, the Barbour records of CT and many other sources. Thus, it has been the primary source for the first 5 generations: Nathaniel 1, 2, 3, Josiah and Jonathan. If interesting but conflicting information appears in other sources, it is discussed in the text).

14. Browne, William Bradford. "Over Pathways of the Past: Familiar Features of our Valley — How they originated — What happened along the way and Pownal Sketches." Printed in the *North Adams Transcript*, 12 Dec 1939 to 9 Apr 1940.

15. Massachusetts Historical Commission, Form 29-3, record of Jonathan Foote House.

16. "Memories of a Little Girl in Pasadena," by Ethelwyn Foote Bennett, published in <u>The Gay Nineties</u> in the 1950s, with copies archived at NEHGS, the Pasadena Library and the Pasadena Historical Society.

17. Wilcox, D.M. <u>Gravestone Inscriptions, Lee Mass.</u>, in 3 parts. Lee MA: Press of the *Berkshire Gleaner*, ca 1900.

18. Gravestone photographs, Lee MA, to be archived at NEHGS.

19. <u>Vital Records of Lee, Massachusetts, to the Year 1850</u>. Boston, Mass.: Published by the New-England Historic Genealogical Society, at the Charge of the Eddy Town-Record Fund, 1903.

20. Massachusetts and Maine 1798 Direct Tax (Online database: NewEnglandAncestor.org, New England Historic Genealogical Society, 2003), (Handwritten tax list, "Direct tax list of 1798 for Massachusetts and Maine, 1798," twenty folio vols plus two suppl vols.) Donated to NEHGS by William Henry Montague, 1850, R. Stanton Avery Collections, NEHGS, Boston MA.

21. Court Records, Book 6, 14 Sep 1784 at Great Barrington, p. 83, from the Knurow Collection, Berkshire Athenaeum, Pittsfield MA, Vol. 35.

22. Danforth, Keyes. <u>Boyhood Reminiscences: Pictures of New England Life in the Olden Times in Williamstown</u>. Gazley Brothers, 1895.

23. Wikipedia.

24. Land records from the Knurow Collection, Berkshire Athenaeum, Pittsfield MA, Vol. 41.

25. Census data, Ancestry.com.

26. Eastlawn Cemetery, Williamstown MA.

27. Consolati, Florence. <u>See All the People; or Life in Lee</u>. 1978.

28. <u>History of Berkshire County, Massachusetts, Vol I & II</u>. New York: J. B. Beers & Co., 1885. VII.

29. Hyde, Rev. C.M., D.D. and Hyde, Alexander, compilers. <u>Lee. The Centennial Celebration, and Centennial History, including Part II, The History of Lee</u>. Springfield, Mass.: Clark W. Bryan & Company, Printers, 1878.

30. <u>Massachusetts Soldiers and Sailors of the Revolutionary War</u>. Boston: Wright & Potter Printing Co., State Printers, 1899, Vol. DUA-FOY.

31. Foote, Solomon, letters to Asahel Foote, Jr, 1824-1828, collection of Judith Bennett Wilson, Providence, RI, to be archived at NEHGS.

32. Rev. Calvin Durfee, D.D. <u>Williams Biographical Annals</u>, article on Asahel Foote. Boston: Lee and Shepard, Publishers, 1871.

33. Perry, Arthur Latham, LLD. <u>Williamstown and Williams College</u>. New York: Charles Scribner's Sons, 1899.

34. Diploma of Asahel Foote, Jr., 1827 Williams College, collection of William Dudley, Washington and Lee University.

35. Asahel Foote, Jr. Original papers, letters, recommendations, etc. to be archived at NEHGS.

36. Maps, including <u>The County Atlas of Berkshire Massachusetts</u>, F.W. Beers, R.T. White & Co., 36 Vesey Street, New York. 1876. pp 15 & 16.

37. Foote, Asahel, 1804-1882, "Farmer's Journal," 1841-1873, HM 66141 The Huntington Library, San Marino, California.

38. www.militarymuseum.org/McCornackGenHosp.html.

39. Asahel Foote Obituary, 20 Jul 1882, *The Adams Transcript*, Vol. 42, No. 36.

40. Elmer I Shepard Collection, file cards, Berkshire Athenaeum, Pittsfield MA. VR and other data re: early Berkshire families, compiled on individual family file cards, mid-20th century.

41. "Map of West Point Defenses," author unknown, published by Pierre Didot: Plan des forts, batteries et poste de West-Point, 1780. (Map of the defense network at West Point, including the Great Chain, Constitution Island, Fort Clinton, Fort Putnam.) Norman B. Leventhal Map Center, Boston Public Library Call #G3804.W53S3 1780, p 5.

PART II – THE SMEDLEYS

PART II – THE SMEDLEYS

PART II – THE SMEDLEYS

PART II – THE SMEDLEYS

PART II – THE SMEDLEYS

PART II – THE SMEDLEYS

PART II – THE SMEDLEYS

PART II – THE SMEDLEYS

PART II – THE SMEDLEYS

PART II – THE SMEDLEYS

PART II – THE SMEDLEYS

PART II – THE SMEDLEYS

PART II – THE SMEDLEYS

PART II – THE SMEDLEYS

PART II – THE SMEDLEYS

PART II – THE SMEDLEYS

PART II – THE SMEDLEYS

PART II – THE SMEDLEYS

PART II – THE SMEDLEYS

PART II – THE SMEDLEYS

PART II – THE SMEDLEYS

PART II – THE SMEDLEYS

PART II – THE SMEDLEYS

PART II – THE SMEDLEYS

PART II – THE SMEDLEYS

PART II – THE SMEDLEYS

PART II – THE SMEDLEYS

PART II – THE SMEDLEYS

www.ingramcontent.com/pod-product-compliance
Lightning Source LLC
Chambersburg PA
CBHW040512290326
41930CB00035B/4